The Spiritual Heart

Diane K. Chapin

Channeling

The Universal Oneness

Published by Light Path Resources.

Printed on acid-free paper.

This book, as are the others in this series, is designed to provide inner spiritual development information and motivation for our readers It is presented with the understanding that light Path Resources is not rendering any type of medical, psychological, legal, or any other kind of professional advice. The works within this series should be considered as adjuncts to any spiritual development efforts in which you participate and you are encouraged to consult with appropriate licensed professionals as you deem appropriate. Our views and rights as presented within this book and series are the same: You, the reader, is responsible for your own choices, actions, and results.

Light Path Resources,
2015

First Edition

Books from Light Path Resources:

Books by Diane Chapin and The Buddha Consciousness (in a progressive series)
1 - A Modern View of God
2 - Living Life Radiantly
3 - Life Through Self Empowerment
4 - A Path to the Inner Self
5 - Life Through Creating Mastership On Earth
6 - Life On Schoolhouse Earth
7 - Spiritual Healing: A New Way to View the Human Condition
 8 - The Light Path
9 - Advanced Keys For Life Management

Books by Diane Chapin and The Universal Oneness
The Spiritual Heart
The Heart, The Pathway of Light

Books by Don Chapin
Engineering Your Spirituality
In Psychic Defense (plus It's a Dog's Life)

TABLE OF CONTENTS

Original
"Spiritual Heart" cover

The Spiritual Heart

FOREWARD by Rev. Diane Chapin

In 1981, I began to channel The Universal Oneness, who helped prepare the way for the guides I later worked with (The Buddha Consciousness - later changed to Quest - and The Physicians). In my quest for self-understanding, it became apparent that new insights, tools and inspiration were necessary.

The Universal Oneness became my source for greater self-realization (over a seven-year training period) in providing the chapters of what was to become "The Spiritual Heart" over a six-month period, starting on Easter Sunday, 1985. It was a most exciting time for me and I want to share these remarkable tools with you.

The Spiritual Heart has a unique message for those of us who wish to greatly alter our lives in a spiritual manner, as we come from a common background grounded in the world's religions of today. The purpose of The Spiritual Heart is to teach us that we are all Masters and that mastership is not beyond the capabilities of the average individual. This is really a self-help book which offers practical spiritual tools for use in our growth and to guide us along the path to mastership. The Spiritual Heart was also offered as a comfort to us along the way, and to let us know that spiritual guides are all about us at all times, we have only to lean on our intuition. Through intuition, we begin to explore the realm of The Christ Consciousness and to become more attuned to the God within. The Spiritual Heart was presented to us to bless us and bring us more light in our life.

The Spiritual Heart was dictated to me in archaic English, which was the way I experienced each message from The Universal Oneness. It is classical in the sense that it reminds one of the Edgar Cayce channelings (who served as an inspiration for this kind of work). While we have replaced such archaic expressions as 'thee,' 'ye,' 'thy,' 'thine,' 'harken,' 'carnal,' 'the same,' and have updated some other occasional wording for easier reading, we have tried to minimize the editing so as not to destroy its beauty and authenticity. As can be seen, much of the sentence structure and terminology still reflects the original archaic English.

I hope you benefit from The Spiritual Heart, as I have, and that you employ the tools it offers. Indeed, that is the greater purpose of this book, to uplift our hearts and to allow our souls to flow into the universal consciousness known as mastership.

Rev. Diane K. Chapin, Easter Sunday, 1985

- - - - - - -

And, yes, to those observant readers, some of our previously published books listed "The Spiritual Oneness" as the consciousness coming through Diane for these two books, but that was my mistake as they actually went by the name of "The Universal Oneness." Historically, however, since the change they have undergone in Spirit, such name differences are now of little import. :-)

Originally, this book had been transcribed from the original tape by an "independent contractor" and published in an 8-1/2 X 11 format (see TOC page). However, the old English pronunciation on that tape was so "thick" that the transcriber had considerable difficulty with both spelling and syntax. So, that first publication had to be re-translated into what this book has become. At that time, it wasn't known that "The Spiritual Heart," as depicted by The Universal Oneness, also had a slightly different meaning, as presented in a later book in this series, "Engineering Your Spirituality."

What I believe is MOST interesting, however, is the quite dramatic differences in delivery between this book and their last one, the next in this series, "The Heart, The Pathway of Light." This book, "The Spiritual Heart," is extremely strong on very basic spiritual principles in a manner and tone quite reminiscent of the late Edgar Cayce, who had so strongly inspired Diane. (In fact, Cayce actually "came through" Diane on, as she had mentioned, two occasions before we met, only one of which she had transcribed, as found in her papers after her transition, and added to this book as an Appendix.) As a result of the activities they undertook to support humanity between their two book presentations, The Universal Oneness apparently underwent a tremendous vibrational shift and an evolution of their own, explained in more detail in Book #11, "The Heart, The Pathway of Light." but the vast difference in presentation styles clearly demonstrates that "something" had happened! :-)

~ Don Chapin

* * * * * * *

"In love and light, we of The Universal Oneness wish you well and bless you each day." "We begin to impart unto thee the secret of the ages, that which must now be given. The Lord our God is upon thee for this most special task. We are about to begin."

* * * * * * *

THE UNIVERSAL ONENESS: Who We Are
(Message of May 2, 1990)

Beloved children, we are The Universal Oneness and, as you may recall, we speak in the dialect of old. We are greatly gratified to once again return to our very treasured vehicle who was so willing to open the door to The Buddha Consciousness.

We speak to you from the feminine energy that we experience as the way of Spirit. We speak to you from an ancient energy of wisdom and grace and we speak of The Christ Consciousness and of the beauty of Jesus on the earth plane. Our orientation is that of Mastership. Our orientation is that of the beauty of Christ's life which, once again, can be understood through the steps that The Buddha Consciousness has provided, but, in addition, through the loving of one heart to the other.

We are here to say to you, our brothers and sisters, that we send you our love and we are here for those who would wish to enjoy our companionship once again.

We, of The Universal Oneness, are part of the All. We are an activity of intuition and Spirit that is available to each of you and we are more easily channeled than a resource such as The Buddha Consciousness, whose energy level is exceedingly high and takes great skill to channel. But we make ourselves available to many through a variety of names and offer ourselves as spiritual enhancers and guides. We are One, but we are All. We are intuitional, inspirational and spiritual, and we offer great love to your planet for its well-being, its preservation and the upliftment of those hearts and souls who have dedicated themselves to the preservation of your planet.

1

We are honored, our brothers and sisters and beloved ones, to have been blessed by your presence, but we will depart now and return anon, farewell, and we say to you, blessings.

Question of June 5, 1990 (before the changes they later experienced): Could you describe who you are and where you come from?

Answer: Let us say this. We are the energy of All-That-Is. We are the voice of universality and unification. We are the 'alteraters' if you will, of patterns. We are the feminine energy in that we are strongly connected to the Mother Mary energy and the beauty of that office that she was installed to as the mother of Christ on your planet. She is little understood for her great spirituality, her striking upliftment and the beauty of her soul. For her young years, she was a markedly advanced individual and was given this opportunity to serve humankind in this way. So, we are strongly connected to her in many ways, but we are not precisely she, for we are more than that, we are an aspect of all elements of all dimensions.

So, we are unification, we are The Universal Oneness. But we are not of the advanced magnitude of The Buddha Consciousness (Diane's main guides). Even though all is One, there are levels. The Buddha Consciousness is the foremost that is available and it is a great honor that you have the opportunity to experience this consciousness on your planet, for it takes a great deal of attunement on both sides to channel such a resource. We are greatly blessed to be working with The Buddha Consciousness to further their efforts and world peace.

* * * * * * *

LIGHT PATH RESOURCES - WHO WE ARE

Light Path Resources is a spiritually oriented organization without religious affiliations, devoted to the upliftment of mankind through accelerating the spiritual development of each individual and answering our quest for our place in the Universe and the God within. Our purpose is to establish a base for each individual, which is centered, joyous, prosperous, stress free, healthy, supportive and which is compatible with the whole physical, psychological and spiritual being.

Drawing upon the spiritual teachings, tools and techniques from The Buddha Consciousness/Quest as a channeled resource through the late Rev. Diane K. Chapin, where many classes, individual spiritual counseling and energy balancing, seminars, occasional workshops, etc., conducted in California, Nevada and Hong Kong, we have assembled the transcriptions into chapter and book form. From these sessions, a total of nine books have resulted from Light Path Resources as listed on the Copyright page.

Diane's earlier guides, The Universal Oneness, who had put her through a seven-year training program in preparation for The Buddha Consciousness, provided enough material for two books, listed on the Copyright page.

See the Appendix of "A Modern View Of God," for Diane's short bio of "'The Vehicle' On The Light Path."

Diane's surviving husband, Don, produced two books, based on our true mutual experiences, entitled "Engineering Your Spirituality" and later, "In Psychic Defense."

From the Light Path Resources 'free church' website, http://www.lprww.us

==================

May your path be light

==================

CHAPTER 1

ALL ARE ONE

The Lord our God, through the divinity of His nature, has seen that the world has come to a place where more can be revealed and explained to those souls who are willing to behold that which is given for their benefit in holiness and grace.

Let us begin with the clear understanding that all are One with God. It is to be understood that there never was, nor ever can be, a separation from God. You may say, "This is known." But the understanding of this is greatly limited, even by those religious orders that teach a more metaphysical understanding of Spirit.

It is time for man to step beyond his human self into the divinity of his true spiritual being. This is the message of all the Masters that, indeed, the door to God is within you. Lift up your hearts in song and praise, for our Divine Father has seen fit to reveal the steps to be followed to receive this information more fully.

Indeed, the concept and understanding of the nature of what is now called the Holy Ghost has been blurred by political assassination, that is to say, by the murder of the truth. Not merely distortion, our friends... but every effort was made to suffocate that which is so dear to our Divine Father. For, indeed, the Holy Breath, is called, She.

That is not to imply the understanding of gender as you know and experience in your slower vibrational plane of action. She represents understanding, compassion, intuition and beauty, for without these aspects, man is little more than a beast.

And so it is, these many years, for the greater part, you have milled around as beasts, struggling for the divinity which you knew not how to achieve, and waiting for the emergence of a male Holy Ghost. There is no such animal, our friends.

By altering the sex of our Divine Holy Ghost by those on the earth plane, the lovingness was removed from that and from man's understanding. For, indeed, as is presently taught, the Holy Ghost is an ominous figure, removed from man and little accessible.

Let us open our eyes to the truth and dispense with this ignorance, for we have come to show you a greater way and to say to you, to all, that it is time for man to enter into his rightful divinity and set aside that which is common.

Indeed, the Holy Breath, The Comforter, is the inspiration that uplifts men. It must be taught and given to the people, to all men as the Master our Divine Lord Jesus Christ, as the Buddha believed in his heart, and as those before Abraham announced to the world: There is only one God, there is only one Consciousness.

The substance and nature of the Universe is spiritual. All things are comprised of the Godself; as within, so without.

Set aside your previous understanding of the nature of Divinity, and understand that it is through meditation and prayer that the nature of Divinity is understood. All who wish to seek a spiritual way of life must turn from the worldly mind and let the Holy Breath imbue them with Her sacred peace.

We do not come to you to speak in riddles, but to open the eyes of the multitude and say that all are One with God. Love your neighbor as yourself and uplift all into compassion and beauty. The organization and teachings of any Master were meant to be patterns for the individual to follow. Discipleship is a stewardship, a living as it were, in and for the Father.

As you grow in awareness of your true nature, old concepts such as 'God is separate and apart,' 'What your eyes see is all there is' and 'Man is not empowered with Divine grace,' begin to have less personal meaning. Your focus then shifts to viewing the world with your inner eyes... through the eyes of the heart.

Intercession Comfort is achieved through the Holy Breath, our friends, for it is She who comes to you to bless you and to show the way to that which is Divine and for all men.

These words are not being provided for merely a few, but for the understanding of all, for many souls have been crying out, now, and their cries are heard. That is to say, there is a longing on the earth plane for the Comforter to come.

It is time for the earth to begin to turn within as One, with that recognition of Oneness with God, through the intercession of the Holy Breath and through the understanding that can be accomplished by individual man. Do not turn aside from our words, but look to that side of yourself which longs for fruition.

All who seek out love from others, seek it to gratify themselves. More importantly, it is, again, the worldly universe's distortion of seeking the Divine love. For, as man turned away from his birthright to live in holiness and peace, to that which is worldly, to that which is material, to that which is of the slower vibrational rate, a gap, as it were, a wound, has been exposed for these many centuries.

The message is, that ALL have capabilities, within, of becoming Masters. For it was that Divine Sonship with God which man enjoyed before the fall.

As he turned aside and gave up the Ghost, man gave up his Comforter, his compassion, his sense of beauty in the Divine and his intuitive abilities. Look about you and know that many seek that once again.

False understanding must now be set aside. This is not heresy, our friends, for to worship a god who does not exist, a god without, is heresy. But that is not to say that will not be set aright.

We come to you to say that each individual must go *within* to receive the Holy Breath. Each must give up the symbology which man believed would lead him to the Father and must come to God as Christ himself, as the Buddha himself, as Abraham... as each did... alone.

Straight the gait and narrow the way. But as each individual trods this path, greater enlightenment for peace, good will and forgiveness are available to all mankind.

One begins by entering into the clear understanding that God lives within, that the body is, indeed, the temple of the living God, and that the First Commandment was handed down that you may come to understand the Divine nature of self. That is to say, "Thou shalt love the Lord thy God with all thy heart and with all thy soul and with all thy mind."

In doing so, a turning away from the worldly mind is automatically achieved, for, as one uplifts in consciousness through study and meditation, one can see one's eyes are opened to the Divinity of self.

The Universal Consciousness is omniscient, omnipotent and omnipresent, as are All; but only through the Holy Breath, our brothers, only through compassion, intuition, love and understanding.

It is time to set aside the concept of male and female as different and apart from one another, for in Divinity, they are the same. "Love thy neighbor as thy self" and understand the First Commandment and the Golden Rule, as you call our just-uttered words, to be one in the same. That is, not to be unkind to self or to others, but to set aside guilt, worries and the punitive ways that man employs to self and others.

Indeed, a peaceful way cannot possibly be achieved until an understanding is brought forth and elicited in all of your Oneness with the Father through the Holy Breath, as well as the love of self and others as One.

This is not a difficult way, but is a simpler way than through mysticism. Understand that mysticism is the understanding and the practice of the Oneness with the Father from moment to moment, to living within, thereby receiving our Father's grace and living by that.

That is walking in holiness, neither looking to the right nor the left, but walking the way of the Father. But that leaves the worldly man in the dust, as it were, and the time has come for the worldly man to begin to uplift, to allow and to prepare for the coming of the Christ, the coming of the Buddha, the coming of Abraham. *The Messiah is within each individual*.

Therefore, our purpose in providing this book is to assist you to enjoy your spirituality in simple day-to-day experiences, because mysticism can seem like a lofty and difficult way of life. In our view, spirituality should be available to everyone through techniques you use daily.

Each tool you consistently apply contains within it the mechanism to increase your life in many ways, such as: Increasing the depth and beauty you experience in your life, gradually decreasing struggle, enhancing your attitude and feelings toward yourself, and expanding your love of God.

The day of judgment is man's judgment upon himself. We recommend that you look deeply within yourself. You will discover that the harshest judgment comes from you judging you.

As you come to understand this, your inner awareness changes and, consequently, your relationship with yourself becomes more loving. As you become more loving of self, the God within becomes the expression of you rather than you judging you.

Our Divine Father does not judge, only man judges self. By this judgment, man sets up his own cause and effect, rather than living by grace. Grace is the peaceful state of reliance upon the Father.

We are well aware that our words may be instantly appalling to some, for the truth often is. But those of you who are appalled the most are directed to look within and, with some effort, you will see that the purpose of the Masters was to give people, ALL people, a way to mastership, a way to their Divine Sonship with the Father, a way to uplifted consciousness. For that, our friends, is the heaven on earth you seek. HEAVEN IS A STATE OF MIND.

Through the Holy Breath, through the loving of our God before all else with good will to men, and through setting aside time in meditation and prayer, heaven is achieved, Nirvana is achieved, Oneness is achieved.

The ancient Yogic ways are, indeed, a means of achieving the opening forth necessary to uplift yourself to receive the Holy Breath, a way to practice the love of the Father through restoration of health unto all men. Through the opening forth of concentrated meditation, greater truth and enlightenment can be received.

However, this is not the only way. Truth and enlightenment can also be engaged through those activities which lead to contemplation, for reverie and contemplation are the forerunners of meditation and prayer.

So then, you begin with the understanding that you are One with the Father and always have been; that all are One in consciousness, love, compassion, beauty and good will.

As you experience this on the slower vibrational plane, it is impossible to understand from mankind's logical standpoint, but is only understood through the inspiration given by the Holy Breath. These tasks, then, are not so terribly difficult, but they are the seeker's duty... and all are seekers, our friends.

Although some seek out in useless ways, some seek out in violence and many lash out at others, seeking that in themselves which they do not understand.

Many turn aside from their deepest longings in the belief that they must flail about and struggle to obtain that which is always available. But that is not given to those who whine and lament, for that is all they hear in their ears, the whining and lamenting of self and of all that is about them.

You must look deeper within. Turn aside from your own whining, lamenting and milling around and do so with a measure of discipline, for it is time for those on the material plane to uplift as One, to walk in holiness and grace.

Much can be achieved through meditation, even once daily as you arise. Meditation may not be a lengthy process, for one only has to acknowledge, each day, his Oneness with the Father and to open himself to the blessing of the Holy Breath... to receive the inspiration to further the growth that the soul demands, and to seek that which is needed for all.

She is available, with relatively little effort, to all those who are willing to open their hearts to greater recognition of the Divinity of all.

We come in peace to show you the way to peace and harmony. But peace cannot be achieved unless there is peace within the heart and a well established uplifted consciousness. It is this upliftment which is so necessary for humankind and can be achieved by all.

More information will come, for the hearts of many are open to this message.

Amen for now, then. Amen and adieu.

* * * * * * *

CHAPTER 2

THE HOLY BREATH

Let the Holy Breath be upon you for this occasion of the second rendering of what is being provided for all mankind.

You who read these words wonder just what it is that can bring you out of your brutish ways and into mastership and the brotherhood of all. As has been clearly stated, the Father is within, without, and all about you. These words are not idle talk, but the presence of the Father must be activated and set forth for the good of all.

Many words are being provided, bringing forth greater activation than, to date, has been done. Many make efforts to realize the impersonal nature of the God force, but the nature of the Divine remains mysterious and unknown, and many are unaware of the true intimacy they share with God. It is God which elicits and brings forth all that is decent in man, for man, of himself, is able to do very little.

The appearance, our friends, is that man is a powerful force unto himself. But watch, daughters and sons, those men and women who look to themselves as powerful will, in time, come to serious naught and often end in great disgrace.

You will find many of those in material abundance have learned how to bring about some usage of the impersonal, universal source. Yet their lives remain in disharmony, as they turn their back on the Holy Breath and those aspects of higher nature which must also be employed.

Before the Fall, man lived in Mastership, divine Sonship with the Father and perfection itself. Now man whines and laments upon the earth's face, believing in an appearance of good and evil. The evil is in the minds of men, for our Divine Father is far too pure to know evil of any resource or sort.

Therefore, as one attains usage of the power within themselves, one must look to those elements of compassion, grace and wisdom, our friends, to find the Holy Breath; and it is wisdom that is harmonizing to the activities of men.

The Father within is ever available, seeking and searching out those who would come under his grace and care, but "straight the gait and narrow the way," has made the task a fearful one for many. Therefore, many stop just short of true awareness. However, there are signs of greater illumination in the hearts of man and many souls are near to that which they seek, but cannot quite find the way.

The way can come into the heart of individual man through organized religion or through the quiet seeker alone, but man must learn a system that allows his understanding to be expanded. We are come to say that it is essential for the salvation of the world and the continuance of the human race that all those who are able to uplift themselves, do so.

Look, now, beyond affirmation and using the God force for personal gain, for such gain constitutes added blessings and follows easily in the wake of your efforts. Hear now, know that the Christ came to show forth all that was possible, for man and his way is the way of the mystic and the prophets.

The doctrine of greater spiritual relations are taught by a few organizations on the planet and great effort is made to bring hope and harmony to man, but the balancing and achievement of the Holy Breath is lacking. Although lives are improved, few are truly uplifted and inspired and it is the inspiration of man that is missing, the beauty that is man's birthright.

The planet was created that all should live in peace, harmony and abundance, and none should fear one another, nor toil to make their daily way. Therefore, this middle way is being given.

The middle way offers man an opportunity to show forth his greatest asset without the tribulation of the mystical life. Those who seek the Father have read these words and know the beginning of the learning to love self and one another without punitive debasement, guilt or sorrow.

It is time to turn away from the belief that there is good and evil. Understand that all temptations come from a belief in the worldly mind and that that can bring happiness and riches. It is time to turn away from the belief that the spiritual way will bring you suffering, impoverishment and possible death, as has been seen repeatedly by what is given in the New Testament.

These fears have kept many from seeking the greater God presence. Let us explain, clearly, that those were times with very few lights upon the earth to show the way. In

17

these last decades much soul upliftment has come about, and the new souls who are making their entrance onto the earth plane at this time are, for the greater part, far more uplifted. Many are quite evolved, for they have come out of love and brotherhood to assist and show the way.

Let us turn away from ignorance and the need to believe that the spiritual way is not obtainable for those of average sensibilities. Nothing could be further from the truth, for the God force is abundance itself, peace and harmony. As you begin to love yourself in less punitive ways, you can only turn to others and know that in Christ, in Buddha, and in all uplifted states, mankind is a brotherhood and all are equal in the sight of God.

You must love yourself and, in so doing, honor the Father. In turn, you must love others as you would yourself and you must forgive.

These, our friends, are prime elements, for the Father cannot flow forth, nor can the Holy Breath move through you, if you are cluttered with resentment, hate, and fearfulness. You say, "These are for enlightened men to do. I have lived in my own way for all my life and feel I should continue, for this is the way of man." We say it is not, but that it is the way of ignorance and stupidity and it is necessary to cast that out.

This can be achieved very simply, but does require continuance and practice. Prayerful meditation is the way. Forgive yourself for whatever you need and each day, as you arise, bring yourself into knowingness that the Father-Mother-God is with you.

For many, actual meditation may be several steps away, but you may begin, as you open your eyes each day, to open your inner eyes by forgiveness of self and others. In so doing, you will feel lighter in heart and Spirit and find your day begins to be a smoother way. These are the activities of God in your life, for the Father-Mother-God will perform all your functions and more easily for you.

At the midday, open your heart... for did we not say the heart was the way to the greater possibilities that lie within you? Open your heart to the wisdom and enlightenment of the Universe and acknowledge the compassion, wisdom, grace and beauty that lies within you.

For, as you forgive, you are practicing honoring of the Father and self love, in its highest form. As you open yourself to wisdom and compassion at the midday, greater happiness shall be yours. As you close the day, acknowledge God as the Father-Mother-God force that flows through you.

Use these small techniques regularly for one year and you will begin to find yourself changing. These are very little things to ask of mankind and very simple tasks that even the most lethargic can achieve. For, as we have indicated earlier, the Divine Father makes the Holy Presence far more available than in previous times and the consciousness of mankind has uplifted greatly.

Mankind's consciousness is in a higher vibrational state and is in more accordance with that of the Godself. It is for this reason that this simpler way can be successfully offered to mankind.

As you do these things, do not turn away from the understanding that a deeper meditation, at least once each day, should be undertaken. You need not fear this alteration from the utterance of prayers by rote, for rote prayers fall on deaf ears as the Father does not recognize any of the iniquities for which you pray to be forgiven.

Once again, all is appearance and is merely bringing those who seem to be 'the worst' to greater understanding of self. For it is their belief that they must satisfy their false appetites for survival in any way they can, that forces these unpleasant entities to be so ungracious.

The time is at hand, and in the immediate few years ahead, when many will live by grace and peace, thereby uplifting those around them... for the Father-Mother-God force was never meant to be held within, but to be shared and enjoyed by all.

Clarity is the way. Forgiveness brings forth clarity. Self caring brings forth forgiveness and forgiveness brings forth clarity, showing each individual his greater possibilities and a greater path for self. For all come with greater feats than are used and all are capable of moving and experiencing these creative possibilities.

The Father-Mother-God created mankind in Its own image, that is to say, in the image of Divine perfection, in the image that knows not the worldly mind, in the image that lives by the knowledge that it is the Father who provides all. This is the image and likeness in which mankind was brought forth and which mankind willingly set aside.

These are not idle words, our friends, for these small techniques will bring you into greater harmony with yourself than you would dream possible. Let us, as a whole and as individuals, look to that within self that has brought forth our words. For we come in response to the cry of mankind for a better way and, we say to you, that that better way is available and immediately at hand.

Honor yourself peacefully and lovingly, with compassion, and honor others as you would yourself.

We pass on to meet anon.

* * * * * * *

CHAPTER 3

THE WAY TO ENLIGHTENMENT

And so it is that, with the upliftment of consciousness, the availability of Mastership is made accessible to many, for all time. Indeed, this comes in preparation for the 'second coming' of our Lord Jesus Christ to envelope this planet as a level of consciousness, an At-Onement, as a fusion of peace and brotherhood.

Once again, the Master comes as a teacher, but with far greater use and efficiency than as an incarnate being and not into such a period of darkness as before.

To that end, it is very important that both genders turn themselves toward that which the Holy Breath gives them; compassion, brotherhood, intuition and insight. It is important for the brotherhood of man and for the salvation of the planet that all bring forth the glory of God through the understanding and initiation of the Holy Breath.

This can never be achieved with continued whining and lamenting, but only through the understanding that is taught in all the major teachings, such as that of grace in the Christian term. However, it is also through the understanding that is not attained by the mind and it is beyond mere metaphysics.

It is the understanding that comes only with the hand of God, the understanding that comes with the turning away from the lower things of man. These responsibilities are upon the shoulders of all.

It is time for man to set aside childish religious differences, for they are only in the way. They are only a manifestation of the worldly mind, of the universal mesmerism that 'what is seen is the truth.'

It is time for man to look beyond the appearance of these false teachings and know that the Lord our God is within self as individual man, as omniscience, omnipotence and omnipresence.

It is time for the awakening of the spiritual man, the understanding that the soul goes forward and that the eternal and infinite way is the way of the Spirit.

You may say, "Too much is asked." But we say that these things are barely enough. For, as you grow into your human adulthood, so too, must you grow beyond that to spiritual adulthood and set aside that which is foolish. You may say, "This is not what I have been taught."

But we say to examine that more closely for yourself, in an honest and open light, and see that the Christ did not come to divide man, nor did the Buddha, nor any other enlightened entity. They came to demonstrate to others what is possible for man.

Our Lord came onto this earth to demonstrate the law of obedience and omnipresence by overcoming the grave. The Lord our God came to demonstrate that all men stand on Holy Ground, are united in the eyes of God and truly, in very practical terms, to one another.

There is truly no difference between dark and light. It is only the understanding that the light always was within and that you have only to open your eyes and see that there never was any darkness.

But many shy away from this truth for they feel that it would blind them. It is just the opposite, for this truth would uncover the eyes and open them to the clarity of the duties of all mankind.

Your duties extend far beyond the Ten Commandments. These admonitions were handed down to a people living in darkness and ignorance, to show a better way, to provide mankind some avenue out of their milling around, to bring out and elicit a far kinder Presence.

This is most important for all, but the mere observance of these Commandments merely make you a kinder mortal, they do not move you one step in the direction of enlightenment or At-Onement with the Father.

At-Onement is to be understood as that which you already are. God lives through you and expresses Itself through you, but not through the 'you' on the lower levels, for there is no recognition of that. Lowly prejudices and separateness from one another must be set aside through prayer and meditation.

As we have said, the way is not so difficult, for many are not so very far from that which they seek, but are confused by what has been taught them (often as children), by their life experiences and by some of the newer teachings that they have embraced.

The way to enlightenment, our friends, is through the brotherhood of man, through setting aside foolishness and the old fashioned idea that there is only one way to God. This is impossible, for God is universal and always available.

God is impersonal. God is not ignorant of your needs, for God is your very own consciousness. God is yourself, your very selfhood. God is all that is good and loving in you and is what brings you forth as even a better human.

All else is worldly mind and foolishness. So, then, how is it possible for God not to understand your needs? The impersonal nature of God is that the Father lives in all, not in a chosen few. Indivisible with you and ever available is the Lord, our God.

You might say, "We understand that the Lord, our God, is the source of our plenty," as the trees and the foliage are in great bounty, as you look upon the earth and see the beauty and expansiveness of the skies, as the sun continues to rise and set... so there is abundance. But it is not the purpose of the Father, to provide you with your daily needs on a command basis. These are added blessings and are given freely.

You have only to align yourself with the universal flow and to understand that these blessings are for all mankind, regardless of their preferences or, for that matter, their ignorance.

Poverty is a state of mind, and never has been anything else. Poverty is a deep belief in the soul that circumstances force one into such a condition. The state of poverty has never been true, only the appearance of the worldly mind presents it as such. We, in Spirit, live in grace and harmony.

It is the harmonizing with the higher vibration that brings unto all the aspect of plenty, and it is merely that which keeps you in ignorance and darkness... the insistence upon living on the lower levels of consciousness and in a lower vibrational state.

Attune yourself. Attune yourself with that which is good. Attune yourself with that which is clarity, for a muddy consciousness can only bring forth confusion. Know, as you arise each day, that the Lord our God, indeed, blesses you; that the Lord our God is your substance, your being, your holiness, your blessing and your very breath of life. Attune yourself as you arise, and know, deeply within, that you merely must give thanks to the Lord our God for the day at hand, for the unfoldment at hand.

You need not make this unfoldment process a confusion, or make it to be a mystical act, for this unfoldment is only of harmony. If you experience anything else, then you know that you are looking at that which is not of God.

Man has long, now, taken a circuitous route to the Father. We say, heed our words, this is no longer necessary and, in fact, never was. But these many years have forced man to the very brink of disaster.

Live not by bawdy and foolish ways, rather, live in harmony. Live in harmony with self and, subsequently, in harmony with one another.

Arise and thank our God for the beauty of the day, the happiness in your heart, and know that, in so doing, solutions are offered. Solutions have always been offered.

But as man insists upon engaging in the lower and brutish side of self, so he has turned away from the Holy Breath which knocks ever patiently at the door of consciousness. Indeed, hourly, the Holy Breath knocks with solutions. Attune your ear, attune your ear to this inner intuition.

Know that you are to be trusted as you stand upon the knowledge that the Spirit of God flows through you. Know, too, that this very Spirit will bring you away from your lower self.

Do not fear the passing of some of your earthly wishes, but, know that, as you become attuned, you will become in alignment with this greater purpose, bringing yourself into a far greater frame of happiness.

These promises are given to all, based upon the fact that mankind, as a whole, is coming into greater upliftment and turning away from that which is, in truth, unnatural.

The natural man, the spiritual man, lives the God life and does so easily. It is only your belief that you must toil (and often in ways that are unpleasant) to make your way, that forces you into a world and a consciousness insisting on the undercutting of one another in order to survive.

Look about you, and see for yourself the toppling of those who live such a low-consciousness life and know that is a universal principle and will always endure.

Know that the natural way is to allow the presence of God to dwell within you as self, as the Higher Self. Man was created in this image, in the spiritual way, on the higher vibrational level of harmony and peace, and in the image and likeness of God, our friends.

This does not have to do with appearance, but as consciousness, as vibration and as the experiencing of that. You experience that in greater blessings, in creativity, in happier relations and, most certainly, in prosperity.

You have only to allow all these aspects to come into your consciousness more fully with the realization that the Father is easily available. The experience of that, is what is necessary now. You need not hide yourself, you know, nor turn yourself inside out seeking a better way.

You need only bless yourself and understand that it is this way that is more natural to you, not the way of the worldly mind. The Masters who walked the earth demonstrated that repeatedly.

Self healing, abundance, omnipotence, omnipresence, omniscience, are of self, but man has insisted upon relegating these to Masters who have passed on from the visible scene and to others who are esteemed in holiness. This is not necessary, for the greater purpose of their coming has then been lost.

Their purpose was to show to all of you, to all of you who live in darkness, that you are Masters upon the earth.

But this mastership cannot be used for evil; that will never be permitted for long, for it is not the harmonious way. It is very simple.

Those who attempt mastership for evil purposes cannot maintain the vibrational attunement and so, of self, will falter, and falter mightily. The vibrational attunement can only be maintained through harmonizing self lovingly with the Father. By that, we mean harmonizing self through the realization that all things that are good and great, are things of the Father.

If you are seeking evil, do not look to use these ways, but look to your own aggrandizement and power. This is not the natural way. It is unnatural and leads man into illness, emotional disturbances, and ultimately into bringing forth unfortunate effects.

As within, so without. If you live the unnatural life, the disharmony about you will tell you that you are living a muddy consciousness. Clarify your thinking and know clearly that for yourself, and for generations to follow, attunement is necessary.

Bring your children up in these ways, in the brotherhood of man, in attunement with the Father at the earliest possible time, for they are very near that. Their joys, their trust, their specialness demonstrates that. They are a sacred trust to all, and should be brought up as the natural man, as the spiritual self, as the embodiment of the Lord our God.

Do not demean or devalue yourself. Hold yourself in proper esteem, but know that the egotistical way, once again, is of the worldly mind. Hold yourself in reverence, always with the understanding that all that is good about you is of God.

Know that the human self, of itself, knows very little of that which is good. If you see yourself misuse this new-found enlightenment to force others to your way for ego's sake, or to set yourself up as holier than another, then know that you have missed the mark, for the natural man automatically demonstrates that which is holy in self, that which is harmonizing of self.

If you find yourself attuning for financial prosperity only, know that whatever financial prosperity that is gained will not last. The permanent harmonizing can only come through the submission of the Holy Breath and to a turning away from the worldly mind. This will not be as painful as you might believe, for, as you live for materiality only, you live in pain.

As you live to struggle your way out of your disharmony, you live in sorrow. As you live to increase your material gains, you often live in desperation. This is not the natural way.

Man was created to glorify the Father. By 'glorification' is not meant subservient holiness. Glorification is living the natural way. It is the flowing forth of attunement with that which is your very self, attunement with that which is the selfhood of all others, attunement with that which is greater than self.

These are the natural ways, and brings forth the glory in all. These bring forth the peace, the harmony and the blessings that mastership, as was demonstrated by the

Masters and the prophets who walked this earth, were meant to be given, were meant to be understood, and were given for that purpose.

Demonstrate, then, the glory of God, not the glory of the worldly mind.

Amen, then. Amen and peace.

* * * * * * *

CHAPTER 4

AS YOU BELIEVE

We continue with this message, beloved brothers and sisters, and tell you it is delivered from the Most High, that, indeed, each of you must take upon yourself the responsibility of self mastery and mastership, for the haphazard ways of mankind, the separation of one from another is a misuse of the Divine use of your being.

In All, there is order and peace; in All, there is harmony and grace; in All there is beauty and imagination.

Hear this: The Lord our God Is One, One with All and instantly available to all. Why would you turn aside from that, for that which is of momentary gratification? Do not turn aside from that which can bring forth all peace, all love, all harmony.

Know that our Divine Father, in His wisdom, passes these words on to you. Mastership is the integration of self with self. By that is meant that mastership is the alignment with self in its highest form. ALL may accomplish these ends and simply so.

Let the enlightened soul shine through the avenue of the mind and the instrument of the body for the glorification of God as was meant to be. Set aside your present fears and your petty belief that, of self, much can be accomplished.

For all who start only for self's gain, in time, are brought to their knees in one way or another, for they have built their false images on the shifting sands of human willfulness. That is _not_ to say that you are to be passive in your endeavors, but it IS to say that events should not be forced.

It IS to say that pettiness must be set aside and replaced with the milk of kindness and the clarity of peace and understanding.

It _is_ to say, that you are to learn to speak the Word, and to speak your word. By that is meant not the pursuit of greater materiality, but the pursuit of that which leads to your greatest fulfillment.

Know that all is possible, but the Divine is the Creator of All, and through of the teaching of the Word, the Father goes forth to make the crooked way straight in holiness and grace. Speak your word for peace, kindness and brotherhood.

Speak your word for upliftment and prosperity for everyone. Speak your word that the creative imagination is brought forward in everyone, in order that those ideas which are of Divine origin are more frequently expressed through mankind. Ideas are limitless and all that is good is of God while all that is not, is of the worldly mind, creating the appearance of good and evil.

Know that there is only good, grace, peace and abundance. Set aside this foolishness of impoverishment. Let not the impoverished look with greedy eyes to those who are not. Rather, let the impoverished look to themselves and examine themselves more fully; realizing for self that it is their own choice.

Let the world seek upliftment in all ways through commitment, through good, through commitment to peace and brotherhood. Let ordinary humanhood drop away from you, and know that can be done without a tremendous struggle for, as we have said, the consciousness of many has been uplifted. The consciousness of many remains at the ready for that which will lead it out of this darkness.

We have come to say, let the words of our Father be upon your lips; look to yourself and listen to the intuitive voice of the Holy Breath to learn the ways that are proper for each, with the remembrance that there is Divine order, and that this order will bring each soul its right and proper place.

Know that the salvation which the Master (Jesus) spoke of was the salvation of each soul coming to terms with self, for no others can save you. However, the pattern that was set down is available if you attune yourself to the higher vibration through meditation, reverie and prayer.

There is no other way that is as thorough, although other avenues can bring a soul with purposefulness and depth to this same greater purpose.

Look not to another to provide for you, rather, look to yourself and know that, as you fulfill your self's purpose, that is the expression of your creative nature and greater resources are made available in all ways.

You say, "What is this creative nature you speak of?" Many may also say, "We have read these words and we know of the creative principle of spiritual law, we know of multiplicity and we know that can be employed."

We say to you that we speak here of the creative nature of the Holy Breath that is available to you through meditation and prayer, and of a willingness to allow that to flow through you. This aspect of creative nature employs imagination and intuitive guidance, for the Father has provided all, that you not walk in darkness, not for one moment.

That creative nature will assist you in harmonizing self with self. Creative nature will assist you in building a more harmonious planet and uplifting mankind from the common ideals of survival of the fittest. The creative nature displays, to all, the activities of imagination, compassion and brotherhood, for abundance is the Divine Way and none need struggle.

As you arise each day say to yourself, "The Lord our God Is One. The Lord our God Is One with All. The Lord our God provides the Holy Breath and I open myself to that creative, intuitive expression. I listen to that and I follow that direction."

These things you do with regularity, and you will see the demonstration of omnipresence not only as your life begins to reflect greater harmonization, but you will find that others about you share this similar experience.

As you see these occurrences, know that the Father is of All; know that the Father is infinite and is beyond the conceptualization of the mortal man.

Do not turn your back on those urges you may have that reveals a better way, and let your life display, for itself, living on the higher vibrational plane. Let each know, for self, that the Lord our God is the still small Voice within; that the Lord our God has never failed you; that the Lord our God forgives instantly.

These words come to you as a new way. Certainly, based on some familiar concepts, but as a way to allow all to participate in that Universal Good which is of God. Not only *of* God, but *is* God.

We say to all you who seek, hear us, and know that the way is in position for you, explicitly so. But know that you are to also give thanks for all to our God.

The choice is yours. If you wish to subscribe that you must whine and lament, that you must crush the bones of others on your way to your imaginary top, if you wish to believe that war is powerful, then know that you are participating in the destruction of your own planet; you are participating against the law that governs the Universe; and you are participating against the laws of good, of abundance, and of peace.

You are then also participating against the God within you and, therefore, you are participating against yourself. Any wonder then, why you over-imbibe, experience ill health and live in the peaks and valleys that can bring you to desolation?

Turn from these destructive ways into the constructive avenue of expressing appreciation to our Father and to the acknowledgment of the God within, without and all about you... that flows through your brothers and sisters wherever they are.

Know that this acknowledgment is to be the way. It is precious little to ask for attaining alignment with your higher purpose and for attuning yourself to the higher harmonizing vibration.

Know that separating one from another merely separates you from your good, and puts off the day when you can look to yourself and know the holiness within you. That recognition can only engender kindness, respect, love for one another and the putting aside of petty human ways, the putting aside of one man being powerful over another. Such foolishness, our friends, is not needed.

Look deeply into your heart and know the sensibility, practicality and, clearly, the ease of that. Know that these brief recognitions should not be overly difficult.

As you arise, look about yourself and know that, as you open yourself to the greater good, each day begins anew with greater possibilities toward the true expression of mankind, of brotherhood, peace and happiness.

May the peace that passes all understanding come to you, that is, the clarity that eliminates confusion, that shows you what is true and correct for yourself and that can only be of God and not of man.

Let everyone begin each day with this clarity, thereby allowing the gracious Holy Breath to be upon them and to express, far more fully, what is correct for each. Listen then, to that inner voice with diligence, faithfulness and clarity.

Know that all is done to you as you believe. Then do not believe in evil, sparseness, sorrow, embitterment with one another, or in separation from one another.

AS YOU BELIEVE... Believe, then, that you are One with God, that that Creative Principal flows through you for your good and the upliftment and good of all.

AS YOU BELIEVE, it is done unto you and it is done immediately, as you believe, with grace and clarity. It is done unto you as you believe.

If you believe in horror, in the grossness of man and that life is an evil and unkind way, so too, as you believe, will it be done.

Believe then, that all can step forward to the higher vibrational attunement. Believe that you may set aside those worldly and lonely beliefs. As you believe, so you will be uplifted, and that upliftment will reveal to each his personal and harmonious way.

Let all be done to you as you come into greater fulfillment, looking one to the other, and seeing the grace of God flowing from one to the other... the brotherhood, cooperation and peace that is the core of each.

Choose, then, how you wish to express yourself, for, as you believe... as you believe deeply and in your heart... all is expressed out for you, reflecting your beliefs. Know, then, each of you must be responsible for yourself... and understand, for yourself, what you have wrought for yourself.

This cannot be altered if you persist in insisting that these lowly beliefs are the way of mankind, for, indeed, they are not... they are merely expressions of brutes, and mankind was created in the likeness and image of the Father; brought forth in His image. That is, brought forth with the Spirit flowing through you to live in harmony and peace.

Those are the images of God; harmony, grace, peace and fulfillment. All else is of mankind and the doings of mankind, for the Father is purity itself and cannot recognize such foolishness. Realize the correctness of these words and take upon yourself a greater responsibility for yourself in cooperation with the Spirit and the Holy Breath.

We are ever with you through intuition, meditation, reverie and prayer. Seek out that which is the highest in yourself and see what greater blessings emerge in all ways. Attune yourself, then, to the higher vibration.

Amen.

* * * * * * *

CHAPTER 5

YOUR PERSONAL COLOR... THE UNIFYING PRINCIPAL

So it is, our friends, that we come to where you now begin to glimpse greater possibilities of proper alignment with Spirit. Indeed, this is the purpose of every incarnation you have experienced and it can be achieved through the ways and means we have provided. You might ask, "And to what purpose does all this dedication lead?"

We say, many are not yet ready for the realization that there is only this one purpose. However, man has come to the earth plane, in the final analysis, for only one objective; that is, to live in harmony as an expression of the glory of God and to do so without confusion, strife, or fear.

The Law of Universal Principle was made available for the use of all, but too few employ it and, when they do, there is confusion and guilt. For many are afraid, in secret that is, and those who profess to understand and make use of it, often suffer, far more than others, the secret fear that they are going against that which is of God.

Let us say to you that Christ came to show the way of living entirely by the grace of God. He prayed without ceasing, meditated long and deeply, and forgave continuously. However, let it be understood that the Christ, in addition to the Buddha and other Masters throughout the history of man, have employed the use of the universal good.

This was given in order that man may learn that he need never fail and it is entirely in alignment with the patterns available for man's use, for the Universe is a mathematically orchestrated sequence and so is all else.

Let us express here clearly that the Law is of God, but it is not God. That is where some confusion lies, for many have interpreted the Law to BE God.

The Law is an implementation of the universal resource of energy, for all is energy, all is composed of energy in different states of vibration and all, therefore, can be employed. The mind of man, for example, is nothing more than a state of energy at a higher vibrational level.

So then, why turn away, shun what is good for you and partake of that which brings sadness and despair? You have only to unite yourself consciously and with the effort which a conscious realization brings with your good, and you will find much flows forth.

Perfection in alignment is available beyond the Law and those who are ready will seek that; but the implementation of the Law must be understood by most before this greater perfection can come about.

Indeed, it was the misuse of the Law that brought about "the fall of man." Man sought the use of the Law for selfish purposes, therefore, separating himself from that which was good, and creating the *false image of good and evil...* for *evil only exists in the minds of man*.

All that has been given is clearly good. But the misuse of the Law brought forth the belief that man must struggle and flail about for survival, at times, on the meanest level. Man then sank to his knees in consciousness and has remained there for some time, doing all manner of despicable deeds and, in so doing, fortifying this misconception.

As we have said, all is energy and all can align self for greater good. You may say, "Sounds very high-flown," as you look to your individual difficulties. Understand that your difficulties only exist in the lower vibrational state. In other words, your use of the universal energies have slowed down so significantly that you have dropped behind your good.

Your good is only ahead of you a bit, then. By 'good,' is meant the resolution to any difficulty that faces you.

What is needed is the clear understanding that it is not necessary for ANY to live at these lower and very slowed vibrational levels. All you need do is uplift yourself from that and many problems will resolve themselves.

This does not even require a reconditioning of the mind or the use of affirmations, although, that method does allow many to readjust to the necessary vibrational level.

What is not understood, is that each individual vibrates at his own particular rate. This is the reason many have not connected with their good, for they look to the good of others, as well as the good they believe necessary for themselves and, in so doing, do not employ a proper connection.

Unification with the proper vibrational level can be brought about very simply, however, this is to be done with the clear knowledge that good cannot be misused.

Such misuse may seem possible for a period of time, but those who misuse their good will sink, once again, into the lower vibrational state and struggle there in that despicable mire. The Law was not given for destructive purposes, but was provided that all may continue infinitely in order, harmony and peace.

Your purpose, then, is to harmonize yourself with your own personal vibration, and, in doing so, a far greater harmony with the Father will be achieved, of itself. Let us say that it was the Father's creation that this personal vibration occurred at all, and the vibration is of the Father.

Harmonizing, then, comes forward with the understanding that all good is of God and that all that appears to be evil is merely the human fallacy that occurred as humans misused the Law. Step beyond that to your personal vibrational state.

Meditate deeply each forenoon in conjunction with your morning meditation as has been outlined on the achievement of unity with the Father. As you do so, know that a color will present itself. That is your unifying principle expressing itself in a way you can visualize.

Visualize this color frequently, briefly and lovingly. This is the key, for, as you harmonize yourself with your personal vibrational attunement presented to you in a way you can comprehend, your upliftment will begin.

As this upliftment takes place, understand that you will find many of your habits and views begin to change. As we have said, the Law cannot be misused for gainful and greedy purposes without sinking back into the fallacy of man's greed and belief in evil.

So then, realize that this is a commitment to upliftment and to greater service to the Father, for many will find new avenues of expression come to them as they set aside old ways and habits.

These things will come of their own accord and are part of the process of unification on the higher vibrational plane. They are not to be feared, but are to welcomed.

Let us understand that the purpose of this message is that the brotherhood of man must be recognized by all. That will happen far more readily if each individual moves into a harmonious vibrational state. In this uplifted state, you will find that there is no necessity to struggle in survival, for all will be provided.

The Law cannot fail you, and the resolution of each difficulty lies in the understanding that difficulties only exist in the minds of men, for universal principle does not even glimpse that.

In other words, as you uplift yourself to a higher attunement, problems will fall away, as is appropriate... for you will have risen above them, allowing the proper answer to be given to you by intuition and even by direct action.

Do not necessarily expect a personal color to be one you have cognizance of, for that is not always true. The

Universe is comprised of many hues and shades few have even glimpsed, for man grovels on his knees and has seldom raised his eyes to look about and see the magnificence that is available, freely and lovingly.

Look to the greater brotherhood of man that the coming of the Christedness in all may be glimpsed and even experienced. That is merely a way of saying a greater demonstration of the possibilities of man, as he strives forward to glorify the Father, is ever available.

Mankind cannot exist in the helter-skelter style of the law of the survival of the fittest, for that only breeds discord, discrimination, distrust and disharmony.

Vibrational attunement reveals the fitness, brotherhood and the beauty of all.

Look to your heart and know the truth of our words: That all can be given, and has been given, that you may come into alignment with the Father with greater ease than has been offered throughout the history of mankind.

Know that our words are true and that the consciousness and upliftment of many have brought forth these words for your use and your upliftment.

Amen.

* * * * * * *

CHAPTER 6

USING THE LAW THROUGH ATTUNEMENT

We are come to bless all those who, in their hearts, are opening forth to the words that have been provided for your assistance and spiritual growth. We speak to each soul who partakes of this book and say, dip deeply into what has been given and understand that there are many ways to approach the Hem of God.

Indeed, in reverence and humility, that should be done, but done purposefully and single-mindedly. By that is meant, know that the law of cause and effect was given for all and for your use.

As you attune yourself to the higher vibrational level, and see yourself, for yourself, in greater alignment with the Father, as you bless and forgive on a daily basis, as you see your health, wealth and your entire life improving, know that these are the harvests of your labors and that, indeed, you have come into greater alliance with the Father.

It is the greater purpose of this work to express to all the immediacy needed for turning aside selfish, puny ways, for they can only lead man into man's greater destruction, rather than into the bounty that awaits all.

Let us say that, as you approach the Father, set all your desires in the hands of the law and come only to the Father for that which is appropriate. That, our friends, is simply to be in the Father's presence lovingly and peacefully and to receive the Father's grace, peace and love.

Know that your earthly needs will be met and often in unexpected ways, for the Father sees all and employs the law to fulfill all that is needful. Let us say here and now, our Divine Father defies all that is human in concept, for the Father is the substance of all, animate and inanimate, and all are One.

This is true, our friends. God is within and without and cannot be contained by the small thinking that man employs. Look deeply into your heart at your previously held beliefs and see how small they are. The Universe is far vaster than you know, or can possibly dream.

We say to you, if God comprises all of that, how can you possibly put your beliefs into these rigid ways that have been given over by petty and greedy men?

Understand that the God of hell and damnation does not exist, for the Father is far purer, by the very nature of Divinity, than man can ever know. It is this purity that is the essence of grace, the essence of your good, our friends.

All good is available to those who are steeped most deeply in the worldly mind as well as to those who trod the higher roads of spiritual enhancement. It is that which is achieved through attunement with your individual color, for, as your soul opens forth, the singing of the Angels can be heard.

By that is meant the Spirit begins to cleanse itself and spiritual discernment begins to awaken in the heart and breast of mankind.

As spiritual discernment grows, it becomes apparent to all the magnificence and magnitude of God. It is not possible for God to live within the confines of the human mind.

Know then, that any perceptions you have held near and dear are inaccuracies and can only act as barriers to greater spiritual enhancement. Know that, as the Universe continues on, eon after eon, in order and peace without chaos, that this is the God way.

The destiny of man is that same orderly progression also; the chaos that exists on the earth merely exists through misinformation and falsely held beliefs.

Man must turn aside from his petty ego and his pettiness in self, and look to the greater picture, that is, the picture of a world united in peace, love and goodwill.

This is the God way, and spiritual discernment is leading many to these conclusions. Many are afraid, though, that if they give up what little materiality they possess, then all will be lost.

It is necessary to clearly understand that man was meant to live in total harmony with the Universe.

Lovelessness and poverty are discordant aspects of self. They are inharmonious. Therefore, they are not of God, but rather, of the little self; that part of self which can only fathom a struggle each day to maintain what has been achieved. Know that all is maintained through God and, as such, is done with order, accuracy and perfection.

We say, then, let that which is greater than you come forth and fill you with discernment and accuracy. Let your eyes and ears be open to the greater truth.

Tune yourself with regularity to the higher vibrational state and know that, in doing so, all of those about you benefit greatly and others benefit far from your immediate sphere of influence.

As we have said, efforts to misuse the law can only result in inharmonious appearances. Let the chaos of the worldly mind pass away from mankind and that peace and fruitage of the Father show itself forth, for it is available to all, and instantly so.

God's grace has never been withheld, nor ever will be, for the Father is not capable of that. Withholding is an activity of discord, and that is not in compliance with the Divine nature. Let that which is Divine come forward in each individual.

As that occurs, each soul will find, for itself, greater fulfillment and considerable lessening of fear as it learns, for itself, that unity is The Way. As each individual learns, for self, that the punitive God that political man has thrust upon his brothers in no way represents the God of love and peace, then he begins to know the one God who brought forth all in order, harmony and peace.

It is our Divine Father's deepest wish that this message bring forth the opening of the eyes and ears of as many as possible, and that all those who can uplift themselves to Mastership, do so.

This can be accomplished by acknowledging that each day flows from the grace of the Father; that each day is an activity of grace in action; that the perfection of nature is a demonstration for mankind to turn away from disharmony; and to offer, to yourself, the total recognition that the disharmonies experienced are not of God nor could they possibly ever be.

Tune yourself with regularity, then, to maintain the discernment that will allow you to shed these foolish notions. Tune yourself to your personal color, and know that by so doing, health, wealth and happiness will automatically improve. Intuitive capabilities too, will begin to expand and bring to each an opportunity to experience the Comforter, Herself, more fully.

Let that compassionate and intuitive aspect express itself more fully and know that Her only purpose is to aid you in every way.

Know that it is the Holy Breath who brings to each the desire for greater spiritual awareness. Listen to your compassionate and intuitive side and know that all is given for the benefit of mankind.

Indeed, all is given for man's use and pleasure, but not for man's misuse and debasement. It is most necessary that alignment begin on the level of each individual as he takes, to self, the responsibility for self.

Look not to those without, but look to that which is within to bring you all that is needed for your unfoldment. Know that need not be a painful and difficult task, for such is not of the Father, but only of mankind.

Giving up the worldly mind for many, however, does not prove easy, for it is a very convincing mirage and, in many ways, our friends, a mirage is all it is.

For, as spiritual discernment enhances you, you will find you can look behind all that you believe important, see the good and the reality behind it, and know that this reality is the truth; that all else exists as a separation from God, the belief in two powers and the consideration that discord is part of the human experience.

Discord's only purpose is the signal to you that you have separated yourself from the Father and that, indeed, spiritual enhancement is needed. Discord serves no other purpose and, once its universal acknowledgment on the worldly plane ceases, it of itself, will fall away and in its place will remain what is purposeful and harmonious.

That is the God way, that is the proper way, that is the way of mastership. As you put forth your foot each day toward attainment of that, you will find the little disharmonies of life passing away. We say, that is needed, that is appropriate and mankind should not exist in any other way. Amen.

* * * * * * *

CHAPTER 7

ACCEPT YOUR GOOD

We have come to continue with our assistance and revelations as to how greater attunement can be achieved, for, indeed, that is the soul's purpose of man's function upon the earth plane.

It is the duty of each individual to look to self and to know that the words we provide are done so with clarity, accuracy and truth. If that is true, then, you have but one duty: To open yourself as fully as possible to attunement with the Father.

Indeed, the saying "cleanliness is next to Godliness" is not merely the cleanliness of physical dwelling, but, more importantly, it is the cleanliness of heart and soul.

If you look to one another with resentment, coveting, or hatred, know that you stand in the way of attunement, your good and your blessings, for all are One. The substance of that which is the Divine Father, Himself, flows through all, uniting all, blessing all.

A soul cluttered with anger and resentment blocks the flow of this precious energy. Cleanse yourself, then, by daily forgiving yourself and all others. Know, once again, that in so doing the deepest observance of the First Commandment is maintained.

For to love self, knowing that self is part of God, uplifts the consciousness into greater heights and out of the mire of that which would keep you immersed in the worldly way.

Know, then, that the steps given are really quite simple, that attunement with the Father need not be the drudgery most have been led to believe, for the Father is very readily available through the Comforter, through The Christ Consciousness, through the Buddha, for all are one.

All Masters who have gone before remain lovingly available to all to bring to them that which is needful, to bring them the understanding of Oneness, for all is consciousness, our friends.

As within, so without. Within, you must deeply recognize the Divine Father as the Author of All and to set aside the foolish notion that evil is of God, for that is not possible.

The nature of God is beyond the understanding of man. Suffice to say, the essence of God is too pure to behold evil as you conceive it in any way, for God is of harmony, grace and peace.

All that is inharmonious is not of the Father, but is of the human misconception of what is real. It is of the indulgence in the slower vibrational rate. It is as if you walked blindly forward, hoping that, miraculously, your eyes would be opened.

It is not possible for your eyes to be opened to behold a truth that seems a fantasy. The order, unity, purity and abundance of the Universe are not a fantasy and that has been made evident at every turn, for you merely need to look to nature and know the exactness of the balance.

Balance is the key to attunement, for it is balance you seek. The greater balance, the more easily the universal good and flow can be achieved.

The spiritual life, in its essence, is a difficult calling, but it is necessary for mankind to daily live more spiritually in each activity and transaction. In doing so, the consciousness of the planet will uplift, which must be done.

Mankind was given free will and the possibility of choice and, if mankind persists upon remaining spiritually childish and looks to the belief of evil and the unkindness of the Divine Father, it brings about devastation and destruction... and more will come.

Free will was given to assist mankind out of his beastly nature, not willfully, but willingly and lovingly. Know that this willfulness on the part of mankind, the assertion of the unpleasantness of life, on the despairing nature of life, on the sadness of life, can only bring about further devastation and destruction.

Look to that which is inspirational, uplifting and peaceful, and know that these activities bring a greater reality into your experience, for that is the true reality, the everlasting reality. All else is a temporary misconception of the nature of good and evil.

Look to the order and vastness of the Universe and know that is the truth; that chaos only exists in the minds of men; that order, peace and grace are the spiritual realities; that spiritual substance flows through All-There-Is with the demonstration of all-knowing, all-powerful, all-present omnipotence, omniscience and omnipresence.

As you make efforts to attune yourself, do not try to grasp or conceptualize the Divine Father in any way, for there is truth in these ways. The majesty of the Father defies the human mind's ability to conceptualize.

Know only that you are coming into harmony with the deepest essence of self, the deepest essence that you have longed for in all the lives you have lived. This essence is that which calls you out of the mire of beastliness, to return to that which was given to you in the beginning... perfection of the spiritual self.

Know that you cannot wish or hope for the institution of these greater values, only that they can occur through the observance of our Divine Father each morning as you arise: Through stating that all is of God and KNOWING that truth; through the visualization and attainment of your personal color, the upliftment of your consciousness into a more appropriate vibrational state and through the cleansing of the heart and soul through forgiveness.

Do these things daily and you will find life automatically becomes far more purposeful, orderly and loving.

Let our Divine Father fulfill all that is needed for you in the ways and means as He sees fit, and in the period of time that is proper. Demanding that all be instantly fulfilled for you, "Otherwise it is not of God," is not particularly true.

The Father fulfills all as is ultimately proper for each soul. Indeed, that is not to say that God withholds, but that the greater view is given. Faithfulness and faith and diligence are, indeed, spiritual purposes, and, in this regard, your task is not easy. For, while it is not the human way to be disciplined or faithful, it must be done and it is always a benefit.

Know, then, that you can call upon the Holy Breath at any time to bring you comfort and peace; that our Divine Father fulfills all as is needful and proper; that you must stay open and receptive with faithfulness in regard to fulfillment, and that what YOU see as a proper way may not necessarily be of God.

The Father works in many avenues and that can never be fully appreciated in the uplifted state. You might say, "Why bother with this nonsense?" We say, if you have hopes of future generations, and the betterment of your present status, if you have an inner longing that is not satisfied, then this is your way.

Indeed, the old ways are slow and tedious and many walk upon the planet who are ready to use a more spiritual way.

Know that the spiritual way brings fulfillment and peace in many ways and that abundance is, indeed, yours. But, before abundance can be given, it must be conceived. One who walks with head down and shoulders slumped, cannot hope to achieve abundance without an alteration within the self.

Abundance has always been available and always will be. Do not look upon those that have achieved that with such distaste.

Indeed, all can live in comfort and harmony, for there is enough for all those who have achieved and have uplifted themselves to open forth to their greater good. But the misuse of that will always elicit the tearing down of that which has been given, for all are gifts of God to use lovingly, not to be used with power and the mistreatment of those about you. Power is of God, and should be used for the benefit of all, not merely the esteem of the small self.

All these things are given that: Mankind may move unto a greater way; the collective consciousness of all may be uplifted; all may see themselves as One and live in greater brotherhood, knowing that the substance of the Father flows through all that is visible and invisible; and that the reality of the Universe is the nature of God.

Order, peace, graciousness, faithfulness and the harmonious way is the spiritual way. That which is of disharmony is not of the spiritual life and should be set aside. Turn your back on that which is inharmonious and remain faithful in the knowledge that all will be provided as our Father sees proper for each.

Do not feel frustrated if you do not receive an instant response, for each soul requires a different tempering. As you uplift more, responses will certainly be more rapid and, at times, even immediate. But that is not the gauge or the yardstick of spiritual growth, for that cannot be measured in human terms.

Suffice to say, "By their fruitage they shall be known." That does not necessarily include how much materiality you can display. Fruitage can appear as wisdom and grace, as peace and love, or as a harmonious life. As that harmony becomes more deeply felt, it will bring forth greater creativity, insight and love of all.

It is through these avenues that the cleansing takes place, and abundance and good can flow forth more easily into physical expression, for all is good and all good is available to all. This has been true since the beginning and it continues eternally and infinitely, without beginning, without end.

Know that your goodness is available to you and that it should be sought, for it is the very foundation of the spiritual way and peace, the very foundation of living correctly and in alignment, harmony and good will.

Good will to all and to yourself. Know that our Divine Father shines forth continually without judgment, without the petty feelings that the slower vibrational rate is an expression of. Uplift yourself, then, and let that which is harmonious and peaceful come to you with grace and happiness.

Until later, then.

Amen.

* * * * * * *

CHAPTER 8

ORIGINAL SIN

We have come to continue with our assistance, for, as has been outlined, our purpose is greater harmonization and this can most certainly be achieved through the ways and means that we have been providing.

There is an area of explanation, however, that will be provided, for it is not our purpose that confusion occur in any way. As has been said, the Law is OF God, but IS NOT God.

That is, the Law is a mathematical sequence, comprised of the careful balancing of energies of the Universe, set down for the orderly progression of all.

We say, do not revel in negative thinking. Do not take to yourself, in a personal way, the negativity which the worldly mind would imbue you with, for it is, indeed, merely that which could cause you some confusion.

You might say, "If one is harmonized with God, why is it needed to employ the Law?" That is, indeed correct, but few live in such a vibrational state as to, at all times, remain in total harmony.

The Law was provided to give man the opportunity of free will and choice. It is up to you, then. Those who can, indeed, should remain in upliftment. But without continuous forgiveness, cleansing of the mind and clarity of thought, word and deed, one is living in the Law, rather than in perfect harmonization.

As greater harmonization takes place, you will find that you naturally set aside the use of the Law. For disharmony only can occur as you step away from the compassionate intuitive insight of the Holy Breath itself.

Indeed, as the concept of our Divine Father was distorted as man sought to live in the mesmerism of survival of the fittest, man forced himself to live by the Law, rather than under the protection and peace of the higher vibrational state.

As you progress on the spiritual path and you enter into the presence of the Father, understand that you may set all desires and outmoded beliefs aside. But, as you do so, clearly know that man is full of desires and beliefs, that the emptying out process is most difficult and sometimes painful, and that many cannot bear up under that. Indeed, the mind often wishes to flail and thrash about unnecessarily.

It is extremely important to understand the nature and influence of desire in conjunction with the worldly mind, for it is that which brings about unwanted illness, horror, lack and poverty. In other words, those deeply held beliefs will be acted upon by the Law, for the Law is of an impersonal nature.

That IS NOT to say the Law is ignorant of your needs, but it IS to say that most consider themselves needy in areas in which they are not. They look to others, they compare, they judge, they do not forgive themselves and they do not uplift themselves through the necessary cleansing of mind and Spirit.

You must cleanse yourselves of false desires and beliefs and understand self, for self. The cleansing of self from false desires does not mean that life about you will not be experienced as happy and beautiful. In fact, it is quite the opposite, for those who live in harmonization find their life flows freely and smoothly without the difficulties others experience.

Cleanse yourself of the belief of original sin, and forgive yourself for that, for that is at the root of all poverty, lack and those conditions that are similar.

Illness comes from a similar notion. Once again, the notion that, "Into each life a little rain must fall," is fallacy, sheer nonsense and completely unnecessary.

Give up the notion that, as man stepped away from God, he forced himself out of plenty and into a desert of impoverishment and survival of the fittest. This was never true.

Once again, those who lived in power, and were greedy beyond the imaginations of most, forced men to huddle in the cold, believing that was done through Divine Action. That was never true.

Divine Action always rights itself, always brings forth the highest good and knows no other way. If universal principle is that of a raised vibrational level of harmony, peace and good... if that is true... how, then, could man be cast aside by a merciful God? That is impossible and was never done.

As man became out of attunement, as it were, it became simple to believe in whining and lamenting, that was man's way. The Law, then, was given for your protection and your use, but man became so steeped in sorrow that the ways and means were forgotten and, indeed, *were not provided to the masses by those who used them for themselves.*

Mastership is man's natural way. As you forgive yourself several times a week for the belief that you are in some way evil, and that you, therefore, deserve the imprisonment that impoverishment brings in the lives that most live, you will find far greater gifts easily flows forth.

For, as you attune yourself, as you forgive yourself, as you listen to your intuition and align yourself with your deeper wishes... those wishes which come through the creative, intuitive way... the Law will be automatically employed for the positive. There can be no other way.

But, as you employ the Law for lowly things, for worldly ways, you will find the way seems to boomerang upon you, coming back to you in a negative way. This, once again, occurs merely because you have stepped out of attunement with yourself.

The Law is infinite... that is, it does not know bounds or boundaries and does not act in a way that you may believe possible, for energy flows through the Universe in many vibrational states bringing, for all, that which is visible and invisible.

Step into the harmony of your personal color, the cleansing of your mind. Live as much as possible in the higher vibrational state. Listen to your intuitive nature with compassion and wisdom for yourself and others and know that the Law will bring you all that is needed... in great bounty.

The Law cannot be employed particularly well for greedy purposes, for that will only bring upon the employer a negative effect. Give up the notion that you are in some way less than you should be, for that brings about self impoverishment... impoverishment of the soul, the Spirit, and the heart.

That is not needed, for spiritual impoverishment reflects itself in many ways and this reflection is not necessarily to be viewed as Divine. The Father does not know of that mean little way to live; a circumscribed unhappy way. Such a way is a reflection of discord.

Let that greater energy supply come to you through the freely flowing channels of creativity and intuition, bringing all that you need, and more. In other words, let it bring you all that you need on both the inner and the outer planes.

For, as we have said, the human mind does not know what is really needed. As the inner needs are met, satisfied and thereby bringing about greater peace, so the outer will reflect the same, without difficulty.

Many forget that as food, shelter and other immediate needs must be met before man could move on to greater philosophical undertakings, so must the inner soul's needs be met before the life reflects greater perfection.

So, when you rave about what you need, listen to your heart tell you what is truly needed. That does not mean you must climb to a mountain top and await the coming of the Spirit to inform you of what is needed, because that takes place right where you stand, now.

One always begins ones' growth where one finds self, no matter where that is, and one looks to self's inner needs and listens to that; for you will find outer needs, if met before inner needs are, can ruin a life. That has been borne out many times on the human plane.

All that is without is meant for enjoyment and your use. But if the within is not satisfied, the without can be an unhappy scene.

Harmonize yourself, then. Harmonize yourself through forgiving yourself and understanding that original sin is only the creation of petty little men. Forgiveness is instant, but you must forgive yourself, you must forgive others and you must understand that *there is no evil, except in the self hypnosis of the worldly mind.*

Live, then, with your eyes open with clarity and understanding that you need not stoop over under the great burden that you are 'not good enough,' for you were created in the image of our Divine Father. That is, you were created as a spiritual entity, as an entity with grace expressing itself individually as God.

If that is true, how can you be full of sins you never committed? Turn away from the belief that man fell upon his knees through the eating of an apple, handed to him by one of the female gender. That was misconstrued and forced upon man through improper belief.

A merciful God provided the Law in the event that, should man step away from total harmony with God, protection would be provided and that, through the implementation of the Law, man could continue to live in far greater peace.

Instead, man forced upon himself the belief that he was evil and that he was forced upon this evilness by the female gender, turning himself aside at that very moment from the Holy Breath itself... from compassion, wisdom, creativity and from the impartation of Divine intuition.

That is at the root of all difficulties between male and female. Look upon that with a clearer eye and you will know, for yourself, that never existed, not in reality. But, as man accepted these beliefs, the negative execution of the Law took place and has gone on now for generations.

Some have found the way out through greater spiritual living, through turning away from negative thoughts and through greater understanding of the Law. But you will find few able to truly use the Law to its fullest. This, once again, reflects some little belief in terms of original sin.

Give up this notion. Once you do, you will find you have no need of the Law, for you will understand that there are no barriers between you and mastership. THAT is the door to the harmonization with our Divine Father.

Uplift yourself, then. Uplift yourself through the cleansing of the soul, and through understanding and forgiveness of self for your belief in original sin.

Harmonize yourself through your personal color, through the acknowledgment of our divine Father as the Creator and Giver of all.

Do your meditations and acknowledgments as outlined, and you will find, our friends, a great burden has been lifted from you, that your soul flies forth and that you live from the within.

As you do so, the without will be easily supplied.

We say, then, do these things with diligence and grace and let the peace that passes all understanding, which is clarity, our friends, come to you... clarity of intent and purpose, clarity of soul, a soul not muddied by resentments, little hurts and the deep belief that man can never be righted with God again.

We bless you, and we depart for now.

* * * * * * *

CHAPTER 9

THE NATURAL MAN

And so, our friends, the greater way has been spread before you, a veritable feast for the bountiful flock. Let us, once again say, the separation from our Divine Father is only in your belief.

That is very much the key to the difficulty of man, for many believe that there is an actual separation, without understanding that there are no barriers to conscious union with the Divine Father. The only barrier is that belief.

For, if you are comprised of Spirit, energy and universal good, how then, is it possible for a separation to exist? There is no possibility of that. It is for that reason that we have come to apprise you that you are not in darkness, nor are you alone, nor were you, ever, for the mercy of our Divine Father has ever been available.

Living by grace, then, is living in the knowledge that there is no task too small for the Law to perform, for many have concluded that the Law is only available for major tasks. That can hardly be viewed as the truth, for, indeed, it was established for your use in all areas, to save mankind from the travail of negativity and the worldly mind.

But, as man insisted upon living through the intellect and turning aside from compassion, wisdom, understanding, creativity and intuition, man realized a separation from our

Divine Father, or, more aptly put, realized a separation from his own good.

Living through Spirit, then, is the understanding that each day should unfold for you in splendor and grace. That is to say, many of the little details, of the little illnesses, of the little financial strains... for those who allow Spirit to fulfill itself as is needed for you within and without... will find that, seemingly miraculously, these areas of difficulty seem to disappear. We say, that is proper, appropriate and natural.

Mankind has turned its back for so many generations upon what is natural that, for many, what is natural seems unnatural. It is the way of Spirit, however, to flow through the uplifted state of consciousness, cleansing it of negative beliefs, and, in so doing, the way of clarity becomes the natural way, the way of grace.

You know for yourself, if you look through anxious eyes with fear and dread, what you fear or dread will be realized. Look, then, upon your life as a moment-by-moment unfoldment.

Begin where you stand and work toward greater clarity and peace. Listen, with patience and diligence, for that creative flowing forth which will take you away from that which troubles you.

As thoughts arise that are new, fear not that these are wild ideas, as it were, for that is the knocking of the creative way, it is the inspiration of the Holy Breath.

In no way can mankind understand the fulfillment of grace, for it often comes in unexpected ways. That is, mankind perceives things in a narrow and circumscribed way, whereas Spirit is formless and, in so being, manifests itself in form as needed.

Once again... know thyself. Look around and within you for self. Know that what is needed, is always given. You say, "But I have need of certain things that seem to be withheld."

Divine Nature never withholds, but, as mankind whines, laments and indulges in catastrophic thinking which leads to natural calamities as well as the institution of warfare, man separates himself from that which is Holy in himself.

For, indeed, what is needed is clarity, peace within yourself and the knowledge that you need not struggle so. That is what is truly needed. All else is easily supplied if you will understand, for yourself, that you must pay attention.

Your only duty is to concern yourself with your immediate relationship with God and to allow that to become a personal experience for you... a personal, realized, and recognized experience through cleansing the mind with forgiveness of yourself and others.

Remember, at all times, that forgiveness begins with self, that charity, patience and goodwill begin with self. If you are punitive with yourself, so, too, will you be punitive with others. Observe the First Commandment as has been earlier outlined.

Observe the cleansing of the mind with forgiveness. Listen with attention to the intuition of the Holy Breath and do not turn aside from those thoughts which, at times, seem impossible.

Know for yourself, however, if you believe that cannot be, then a catastrophe must occur, because that has always been your experience. Then you are blocking that which should be so simple.

For, as man has struggled, whined, lamented and fought its way forth from this negative thinking, many have come to realize that there is no catastrophe other than that which one holds within the self.

Listen to your heart song, that is, listen to what is within and is true for yourself. Know then, that destructive ways, catastrophic beliefs and fear must be set aside. Know that there are certain, specific steps which must be followed to open the way for your realization that you were never separated from our Divine Father, and that such a thing is impossible.

If you persist in haphazard and pointless ways, however, you will not find your good evidencing itself. That is not to say, our friends, that improvement does not take place, indeed, it does.

However, we speak of enormous change, of considerable improvement in the health, wealth and well-being of the within and the without. Be assured, you must come into balance within in order for the without to evidence that harvest.

These are comparatively simple ways and means, our friends, that will accomplish a considerable upliftment for all. For, as you live with greater personal integrity, clarity, and peace, so those about you will come under greater personal well-being.

So then, know that negativity and catastrophic thinking, anxiety and fearfulness, the belief that you must toil at menial tasks that do not satisfy nor please you, are not natural. For it is this forcing of self into unnatural ways that brings about illness.

The natural man lives a far more healthful life and is radiant from the Spirit within. The natural man does not indulge himself in anxious, fearful thought, for he remains constantly attuned to the vibration within.

The natural man ever listens for the whisperings of the Holy Breath which will lead to what is needed, to the answers that you seek for all your difficulties. For there is always a way, our friends, although the way may not be apparent, or, for many, may not even seem possible.

The natural man realizes his Oneness with God, looks about the vastness of all and knows that there are no impossibilities.

However, mankind has been so thoroughly imbued with his beliefs that it is difficult for most to live in this more natural way. What must be done, then, is a continuous realignment with Spirit, with the uncovering and setting aside of these many foolish beliefs.

What must be done, then, is to look into self and to see your natural way. That is the spiritual way, the peaceful way. To understand that is not disturbed thinking, but natural and correct.

You may say, "We have lived this way for generations and it seems natural." However, we say that if you persist in such foolish thinking, you turn your back on yourself, on all that is good and gracious.

You say, "I have attachments to my beliefs." But we can assure you that these attachments hold you to confined and limited thinking, and keep you bound in constriction, confusion and grief, as it were.

Your inner rebellion, your inner feeling that you toil and labor under unbearable burdens, are truly the knockings at the door of consciousness.

Listen. Listen within. Know that those feelings are the feelings of one who lives in constriction against all that is natural.

Those are the feelings that one would wish to express in a natural and proper way. You need not live in anger, resentment and bitterness, rather, live in peace and harmony.

Many are thrust into areas in which they are not suited, in relationships, employment, and ways of viewing themselves and others through their continuous belief in survival of the fittest. But the natural way will take you out of that confusion and desolation.

Let the Holy Breath lead you out of those beliefs and into a greater harmonization with Spirit. It is through this greater harmonization that At-Onement with the Father is realized for self.

All our words can fall upon deaf ears if you are not ready to set aside most of what you believe to be true, for it is through forgiveness, the cleansing of the mind, harmonization with personal color and release of anger and resentments, that allows greater access of Spirit to flow forth. Although it is most difficult for Spirit to flow forth when one's consciousness is so muddied yet, indeed, Spirit still does.

Many times much good is offered, but the way seems unnatural or fearful, because mankind lives within the narrow parameters of anxiety and fearfulness, and the greater way is allowed to pass out of visibility. That is to say, opportunities are passed over and opportunity, our friends, comes in many forms, not just opportunity for financial betterment.

Often, opportunities come in ways to repair your relationships, to uplift yourself, or to bring yourself into greater balance. However, the unnatural man turns away from these opportunities, back into the fearful way, hoping that, by some magical means, all will be uplifted and lifted from him.

There are no magical or mysterious means, our friends, but there are definite necessary ways to allow your good to come to you. These are the ways of the natural man. And, as you now know for yourself, there is no mystery in that.

We say, then, live with your ear attuned to the whisperings of the Holy Breath. Live in the deep self awareness within that you are Spirit, that you are One with our Divine Father, that all boundaries are unnatural, that you can set aside the anxiety, the rebelliousness and the resentment that you labor under.

Indeed, you can set these all aside and live from moment to moment and from day to day in the natural state and allowing Spirit to flow through your unencumbered self, bringing you precisely what you need and in great abundance.

So then, listen to our words and let our Divine Father make His Presence felt with purity and grace. Let that flow through you as an avenue of upliftment... for all are One.

All are created in the image of Spirit, that is, in the natural way, the way of harmony, peace and beauty. Let that be a boon and a blessing to you and turn aside from the unnatural man. We meet with you soon, then, and say,

Amen.

* * * * * * *

CHAPTER 10

THE LAW OF NOTHINGNESS

We have come now, once again, to continue our message of eternal truth, for it is that which you all seek, here and there, and so blatantly miss the mark.

Indeed, all are blessed and walk in holiness, but few respond to the continuous knocking at the door of consciousness of the Comforter, who seeks to bring to all of you the intuition, harmony, grace and peace of an abundant Universe.

Stop yourself when this knocking occurs, listen deeply, and open your heart to that, for it bears the harvest of forgiveness (which is peace), the harvest of honesty (which is growth), the harvest of clarity (which is alignment), and the harvest of passivity in the face of resistance and negativity (which is harmony and prosperity).

We know these things are of great concern to those who dwell on the human plane of action. This is most significant, for many seek harmony in the material way only and that is not possible.

As you apply what has been given, know that if all you seek is for material gain, it may come for a time, but it will not be long lasting, for permanent attainment only takes place in what is rooted upon the solid grounds of a spiritual way. By that is meant clear understanding of the law of nothingness.

This is confusing to many, and many fear that, if they walk into nothingness, all that is of material comfort will, of necessity, drop away. Indeed, this may occur.

However, let us be clear, and say that nothingness is the way of peace, clarity and enlightenment. Nothingness reflects the clarity of all the Masters, for that implies one who has stepped well beyond the worldly mind... one who knows that, in order to be fulfilled and filled, you must first be empty. Indeed, a vessel cannot be filled that is already filled with negativity.

Nothingness speaks of the understanding that the reference is made to negativity, for negativity fills up that space which nothingness should occupy. That is to say, the time shall come when you will look deeply into yourself and know that nothingness is the way.

This can be achieved more easily than you would believe and, in the comfort of nothingness, you will find yourself aligned with all avenues, ways, and means opening forth for you. For nothingness is the lessening of desire, and mankind is filled with that.

Many believe that desire is the impetus to success. However, desire also is the foundation of negativity. For, as you desire, the conflict begins and the belief in original sin and survival of the fittest becomes the way.

Desire fills mankind's emotions and colors them so greatly that most cannot see beyond them to the reality and the knowingness that absolute clarity, revealing itself in nothingness, is the way.

Desires clutter the mind, casting a shadow, a veil, over the truth and the way. For, if you desire and it rules your way, you will find little time for upliftment and acknowledgment of our Divine Father as the Author of all good.

In the healing of desire, the belief is fostered that the author of good is self. Desire imbues self in many areas and floods the consciousness of mankind as though it were merely a sponge.

Know that your desires run you into conflict. If you would put them aside, you shall find all that is needed, and considerably more, flowing forth.

You might ask, "If I lose desire, how will I know my way?" The way of the world is that fraught with desire, and creates conflict and difficulty. Stand on your spiritual principles, then, and know that desire should be released on a daily basis.

At midday, then, when you harmonize yourself with viewing your personal color, unconsciously bring yourself into alignment and know that desire blocks spiritual alignment, and greatly so.

Know, for certain, that through the Holy Breath, through compassion, wisdom and intuition, a greater creative way will flow forth, rather than a way dragged down by negativity. Do not let desire clutch at you, as it would so willingly do.

Rather, harmonize yourself with the higher vibrational plane of love and peace, and know that, as time passes, you will find desires, of themselves, falling away. This is needed to replace that which is negative, worldly, and unholy.

This, indeed, requires a clear understanding that setting aside of the human ego is, indeed, a necessity. The ego seldom functions as a positive, for it keeps you tied to the foolish belief that you are the author of all, good and bad. Man, for man's self, can do very little for self, of self.

The greater Author, our Divine Creator, is the Author of all that is good, for our Divine Father is too pure to behold the iniquities and desire-filled ways of mankind. Rather, mankind, in his desires, is the author of the negative experience that befalls him.

If you live in poverty as you read these words, know that you have produced that for yourself, for you stand deeply imbued with the negative way. Know that a more positive and gracious way must come to you and that you must rid self of hurts, resentments and the belief that those who seemingly lack for nothing are, indeed, not your betters.

True prosperity is an uplifted and fulfilled life, that is, one in which all aspects are in balance, harmony, health, peace, abundance and prosperity.

So, then, do not look with greedy and desire-filled eyes to those who seemingly have; rather, release the envious resentment and uplift yourself in order that a greater way be made clear to you. Know that your upliftment out of depths of desperation begins with yourself and not with another.

If you live well, you may say, "Well, then, I need not look to these ways, for clearly now, these ways are for the poor." Such thoughts are of a foolish heart and can only bring you to your knees in despair.

For, as you live in the negative way, you are daily, hourly, turning your back on the universal principles and, instead, insisting upon living by the law of survival of the fittest.

In its own time, this law, of itself, must bring a negative influence into that which you believe you have produced for yourself and your ego. Know, then, that if you would but empty yourself of the belief that nothingness brings poverty and sorrow, you would find yourself fulfilled with thoughts of a far loftier purpose. In other words, your consciousness would begin to uplift and so the consciousness of others about you would do the same.

This is a necessity for the continuance of your planet. Let yourself be fulfilled and you will find that you no longer toil in a drudging way for all that you believe that you need.

Rather, the heart's way, the purposeful way, the harmonious way of each soul's direction and purpose is opened forth and this takes place in the atmosphere of nothingness. This is a most arduous and difficult goal for those on the human plane to fully achieve.

However, all efforts at setting aside negativity and the worldly mind will be of considerable benefit in ways seen and not seen, for, once again, those who are filled with desire only anticipate that which is seen, felt, and heard, and often much is missed.

In that way, you are skating on the surface, as it were, never truly touching upon the real possibilities of mankind; the possibilities that bring forth total freedom... that is, the freedom from negativity and the beliefs in original sin and the law of survival of the fittest.

Turn away from the desire-filled way, and know that will bring you a great blessing, peace, love and continued harmony. Do not let the worldly mind cloy and grasp at you... and that is a continuous effort on the human plane.

Spiritual principle and understanding must be ever advanced, for the consciousness demands that now and it is being given you to assure you a greater way. Nothingness is the opposite of desire and is the ultimate in spiritual growth.

Therefore, do not despair, our friends, but know that you progress toward that in an ever continuing flow which will bring you into harmony with all that which is of the Universe.

If you are full of earthly desires and thoughts, harmonization cannot take place, for within nothingness lies the possibilities of mastership. Turn aside from your desires, and know that, as you do so, all that is not needed will fall away, much negative thinking will pass from you and, of its own accord, considerable improvement will spring forth.

Nothingness is the way of progression to alignment, harmonization and reconciliation with our Divine Father. Do not despair, our friends, but accomplish this task on a frequent-to-daily basis.

Know that, as you harmonize yourself with your true and personal color in a loving and useful way, each day, you progress toward the nothingness, which is All. Meditate deeply, rise above your desires, then look back upon them and know, for yourself, the meaninglessness of those desires.

It is this illumination which will bring you into the knowingness and certainty that this is correct. Do not fear the emptying out process, for it will be immediately fulfilled with a better way, with a purer and cleaner way, not fraught with anger, resentment, bitterness and the willingness to step on your brother; for nothingness is the basis of brotherhood, peace, love, and alignment with all that is possible in the Universe.

So then, know that a far greater way comes to you, a purposeful and proper way. Hear these words and know that they are given in holiness and peace.

We say, Amen, then, and blessings upon you as you trod this sanctified path.

Amen, then.

* * * * * * *

CHAPTER 11

LOVING YOURSELF

We have come, now, to continue our discourse in alignment with our Divine Father. We say that this is of the utmost importance for all and should not be shunted aside as an inconvenience.

For harmonization brings about all that man has sought, all that the unnatural man views as a dream, all that the unnatural man whines and moans and even gnashes his teeth over in unnecessary frustration.

The way to our Divine Father is, most certainly, through the door of forgiveness, harmony with personal color and, surely, the consideration of one another as you would wish to be considered for yourself... the Golden Rule, as you call it, is a great key to harmony among all on the planet. All is consciousness and all that is good is of God. All else is of man.

Indeed, this must be understood as an opportunity for the Soul to come into balance, grace and harmony. It is, indeed, the disease of the soul to be out of harmony that causes much stress in life, opening the way to greater illness and, certainly, causing many of the emotional disturbances that are commonly suffered by many on the earth plane.

Indeed, it is the comparison of one to another, the judgment of that, the looking to others rather than to the Most High, that brings about considerable disease and neuroses, that brings about considerable emotional turmoil and inability to maintain a steady, centered way of approaching life.

That, our friends, is very much the message: Stay centered in God and focused on love, forgiveness, abundance and peace. Recognize that your correct direction from within, listening to the Holy Breath, allowing of the creative force to bring you a far greater lifestyle and way of being, is all provided for you.

As more souls come into harmonization and alignment, far more beauty, creativity, and information for all will become available. The possibilities of man are, indeed, endless, and the vastness of our Divine Father, of the Universe, is greater than man has yet perceived. That is to say, great assistance is offered to you, so do not turn your back on that merely because what has been said is new or different than you have been taught to believe.

Understand that man incarnates for many purposes, but most simply the purpose of eliciting greater knowledge of universal spiritual truths for the soul's growth, is most important, and, indeed, the way to greater happiness for all on your plane of action.

Although, by most, poverty is viewed in terms of funds, there are many levels of impoverishment and those who live without the sustenance of grace, the whisperings of the Holy Breath and the blessings of our Divine Father, live an impoverished life, for very often that life reflects influences of destruction and unhappiness.

Balance, then, is what you seek, spiritual balance. This can never be achieved without first acknowledging our

Divine Father as the Author of all that is good and recognizing the enormity of that.

Know that grace is always in action, always available, and always of great abundance. You might say, "That seems very far away." We say that it is nearer than your hands and feet and closer than breathing.

For within yourself is a temple of the Living God, and it brings forth, through meditation, prayer, forgiveness, through an attitude of listening and of knowing yourself for yourself, a greater way for each individual.

Let us say that it is far easier to take on the personal responsibility for one's spiritual development than to run through one's incarnation in a scattered condition, at the mercy of the winds that blow you about, scattering you in many directions, sapping your energy and your peace.

So, then, look to the way that has been provided. Know that it is a blessing and that it has been imparted for all who are willing to understand that all is of Spirit, and to look beyond the very convincing appearance of the material world.

As you pass through the door of death, all materiality disintegrates, as it were, and falls away. Note the spiritual treasures of observance of the First Commandment, "Thou shalt have no other gods before you." None, that is to say.

However, many worship the God of abundance for abundance' sake and even health for health's sake. Many worship the God of filling self up with objects, the true cause being spiritual imbalance.

Indeed, spiritual balance is the key to all that you seek, for you know that no task is too small for Divine Action to perform. Know that the law was given for your assistance and protection. That should be clearly reviewed, understood and, certainly, employed for your benefit.

Do not fear that the balancing and the setting aside of old ideals will be so excruciating. Rather, look to what truly is difficult and excruciating, that is, the haphazard ways of man that brings forth such calamity and disaster.

A consistent willingness to listen to a higher voice within yourself to bring about greater personal harmonization and, consequently, of the planet, is the spiritual way. This is a very simple plan, our friends, and certainly one that even the most sloppily disciplined can manage to accomplish.

This is for your benefit, your upliftment and the enhancement of your current and subsequent incarnations. As has been said, patience, love, gentleness and forgiveness are the ways and means to balance, to what you would wish to call salvation.

Salvation is within self and through self, and does not come through another, for it is the balancing of the soul and bringing these attitudes forth on a deep level. These ways and means are yours for eternity, whereas all else is of a very temporary nature.

In other words, our friends, take the responsibility to look to yourself with a greater range of view, that is, view yourself as an eternal being, as a spiritual being and, indeed, as a loving being, for love is the key to all.

Love, indeed, is the answer. Know that your love of God, the living for self in less punitive ways, will bring to all the way of responsibility for self. In the final analysis, it is up to you. It is up to you to stop your whining, lamenting and haphazard ways.

The door of death awaits each individual at the end of each incarnation and is merely a crossing over and shedding of a physical body that is no longer necessary. It is the moving forth from one plane of action to another and, indeed, it is the soul's opportunity to review each incarnation and to know, for itself, what balancing has been achieved.

So, then, to run about collecting objects, hates, jealousies, resentment and unhappiness is greatly detrimental to self in the truest sense, for these aspects remain with you, and require additional balancing and greater spiritualization of thought. That is, all these lowly ways can only bring you into additional incarnations to work them out for yourself.

Do not set your spiritual responsibilities aside, then. Rather, know that each of you must decide, for yourself, when spiritual impoverishment will cease and bring yourself to the greater way.

So, then, heed our words and take up a meditation as you arise, at mid-day... no matter how brief... and before you retire, to bring yourself into the harmonization which is so necessary.

Spiritual adulthood is indeed lacking on the earth plane, but, as has been stated, is not so difficult. Let these ways and means bring you all the comfort, peace, love and grace that is ever available.

Set aside spiritual impoverishment, for that is the basis of poverty, of lack in health, wealth, peace, and happiness. Take the responsibility to correct that and bring yourself into alignment, harmony and grace.

Uplift yourself, then, out of the mire of desolation. Look to that which is in you that guides, strengthens and is ever available for your every need.

Do these things, our friends, with ease and grace. See for yourself that these are principles that, indeed, are not abstract concepts; rather, they are working ways to bring all out of desolation.

Take the responsibility to recognize the truth of our words and not to set them aside. Review what has been said, carefully, before you turn aside and return to the old ways. Know that your consistent efforts will open many doors and uplift you to the peace and comfort that you seek.

Peace and love, then. Amen.

* * * * * * *

CHAPTER 12

BROTHERHOOD - THE SPIRITUAL WAY

Our friends, we have spoken to you of your responsibilities toward yourself and, indeed, toward others. All are responsibilities toward our Divine Father.

All are your responsibilities toward God, as it were. For in whatever path you may choose to walk, you must recognize the Father as the Author of all that is good and prosperous and to know that all else is of the worldly mind.

So, then, your only responsibilities, your only duty is to release, bless, and forgive, as regularly as you can, and to loose self of all pettiness and resentment in order that the grace of our Father may continuously flow forth, and that you may see, for yourself, the beauty and grace of this more proper way of being. For alignment, through forgiveness and visualization of your personal color is, indeed, the way.

You must know that all begins with self and that your personal salvation comes through self alone. For, if you are filled with unholiness, that is, if you are filled with hate, envy, jealousy, or resentment towards yourself, toward others, toward any of mankind, you debase yourself in the fullest sense and stay trapped in the petty ways of survival of the fittest.

It is the duty of all who inhabit your planet to release and forgive, to bless one another and to uplift self as much as possible.

It is only in this way that the sadness, violence, the many catastrophes that beset you, can possibly be set aright. Indeed, otherwise, you hurtle yourselves forward to greater negativity, which can only surround you with fear and darkness.

Let the upliftment of mankind become the duty of each in the knowingness that, in so doing, each and every life becomes improved and enhanced. That is the way of mastership.

Mastership is the way of peace, clarity and solidarity. A house that is built on the shifting foundation of sand can only collapse of itself, but a house that is built upon the rock of our Divine Father, is a sturdy and prosperous one. Plant your seeds of love, hope, prayer, forgiveness and beauty in the garden of Divine Love.

Know that, although it may not seem natural to you, some uncovering and looking to yourself with greater honesty will reveal, for yourself, that it IS natural, and that peace, clarity, abundance, love, beauty and prosperity are the natural way.

That is also the proper way, the harmonious way, and the way of harmonization with Spirit. That cannot be achieved if you are filled with the need for survival of the fittest and the belief that the worldly mind is the avenue of truth and reality.

That is the message this day, our friends, look beyond, far beyond what you perceive as real, and understand that is of a very temporal nature; it drops away from you immediately upon the passing of death's door and, indeed, the realty of the spiritual nature of the Universe becomes apparent.

Know that on your side of the veil, the knowledge still lives within you that all is spiritual, that reality is the spiritual way, and that this whining, lamenting and insistence upon needs that can only fill you with vices and eventual destruction are not real. That is to say, these needs are not eternal.

Reality is the eternal way, the way of mastership, the way of forgiveness, the way of not binding one's soul to another and the way of balance and love. These are eternal gifts and treasures and should be treasured above all else, for they are truly the coin of the realm.

The worldly mind insists that, if you are to successfully survive, you must walk over the bones of others, you must be unforgiving, you must fill yourselves with more than is necessary and you must lock yourself away from the comradeship and companionship of others because, perhaps, they seem different, and their brotherhood is the way of weakness.

Nothing could be further from the truth, for it takes strength of character, foresight, discipline and understanding of a far greater nature to see that brotherhood and forgiveness are the reality. If you have difficulty grasping that, simply look to the pettiness of the worldly way, the meanness, the punitive aspects and the grief it brings, and you will know that could never have been of Divine origin.

They are the origins of misbelief. They are the origins of confusion and disorganization and, indeed, they become the origin of destruction, be it in sickness, financial loss, loss of relationships, loss of self esteem, or in national war. All are founded on the belief in original sin and survival of the fittest.

You are given an incarnation to work out certain aspects for yourself, and, indeed, to see the greater way, the way toward harmonization with the Father, the way toward peace, love and understanding. This is very important and, indeed, the importance is personal to each one of you.

You may say, "I am not my brother's keeper." In the spiritual way, each entity is responsible for itself, but in turn, each entity must turn within to uplift self, to bless self, to forgive self and others and, in so doing, further the upliftment of the planet. In that sense, you are, indeed, your brother's keeper, for you are responsible, individually, for the carnage that you have wrought.

You are responsible individually to uplift yourselves and to bring a greater way to the earth plane. You say, "If I spend these hours, even minutes of devotion, I am spending time away from my family and my life which needs my attention." That is a message of ego and, indeed, only bespeaks the foolishness of the ego.

For, if you would but truly experience alignment with our Father, you would find far greater ease comes to you and many of the small difficulties you view as mountains would drop away... for greater health, peace, love, abundance and happiness are available to ALL. But EACH must take upon self the responsibility to open the way and to know that no one else will accomplish these matters for you.

It is up to you, then. You choose. Choose, for yourself, the way and whom you will serve. If you choose to serve through the whining and lamenting, the worldly way, you can know, for a certainty, that the way will be filled with barrenness and rockiness, for that is the harvest of negativity.

If you choose to be responsible for yourself, to be a spiritual adult, to do the very simple meditations which have been given and to do so with consistency and diligence, you will find the reality behind that. You will find a far more solid foundation for your experience and a far happier, more loving, life experience will open forth.

You need not examine each petty detail of your experience for, through viewing your personal color and allowing alignment to naturally flow forth, much will be washed away in that healing, forgiving, blessed light. That is the light of our Divine Father, the light of clarity, of peace and joy. It is also, indeed, the light of prosperity.

Let this light shine for you in radiance, joy and glory. Let this light show you the way. Let this light be your guiding light and come to you as honoring our Divine Father in all your ways.

Know that, in doing so, you rely upon the Holy Breath, the voice of wisdom, compassion, creativity and love. This, indeed, is the reality of the eternal way, the reality of infinity and the basis of all that you seek.

All else merely provides you with distractions from the truth; that there is only one God, one consciousness, one self. Know that, as you debase another, you greatly debase yourself. Look upon your brother, then, with compassionate eyes, as you would have your brother look upon you.

Know that, if you will keep this vision, this understanding of how you would wish your brother to look upon you, you will find yourself viewing your brother differently, with more peace and love.

Those so-called differences from one entity to another are merely those aspects that are taken upon self in a given incarnation to work out. They are not the totality of that entity, for the totality of each entity is spiritual.

Look to the reality, then, of the spiritual way and the simplicity of that. Do not be frightened by that simplicity, for, indeed, survival of the fittest does seem a complicated way.

The order, clarity and peace of the Universe is not complicated. Set aside your need to be busy in strife and struggle, and let yourself find the harvest of His greater way.

Once again, we say, it is up to you to be responsible for yourself and to uplift yourself. You choose the way in which you would wish to walk. If you choose materiality, know what it will bring; if you choose self mastership in the Divine Way, know, too, what your choices will bring you... the peace of mind you each seek as you whine, lament and rail against a God that would treat you with such lack of compassion.

Know that it is your own misunderstanding that leads you to such a lack of compassion in your view of our Divine Father. Our Divine Father is, indeed, a merciful and loving God and has provided you with every way possible for ease and comfort in your experience on the earth plane.

Each soul is repeatedly given the opportunity to redeem itself in looking to the greater spiritual reality of the nature of the Universe through forgiveness of self and others.

Choose, then, what master you would wish, whining, lamenting and haphazardly flailing about, or the way of mastership, the way of harmonization, peace, prosperity and the honoring of our Divine Father.

That is, knowing that our Divine Father flows through all and is available to all at every turn, closer than hands and feet, nearer than breathing. Our Divine Father has never left you nor forsaken you.

Do not turn away, then, from your every benefit, but turn within and know the harvest of spiritual adulthood and responsibility. Release and bless all. Look with clear compassionate eyes on the suffering of others and uplift yourself above that.

See the eternal way of the Universe. Let that flow through you and move you into a more enhanced way of being. Bless and forgive yourself, then, and be at peace.

We move on, then, our brothers and sisters, and say Amen.

* * * * * * *

CHAPTER 13

THE NATURAL WAY

And so, our friends, as you can see for yourself, what has been provided is given to you as a means of greater attunement and recognition of the truth and the knowledge that lies within the breast of all. For, indeed, if you will but listen to your heart song you will know the truth in regard to self.

Many may say at this point that, "Although an inner recognition of spiritual responsibility and duty may be appropriate, that, indeed, our day-to-day efforts in the struggle to control what continues to be a difficult environment on the external, take up almost all of our time and, indeed, all of our thoughts."

We say to you, then, all changes that are brought forth occur within self, before they ever become evident on the outer plane. This occurs for you every day, even without your recognition, for spiritual laws are ALWAYS in effect.

Our Divine Father is ever infinite, ever operating, omniscient, omnipotent, omnipresent, omniactive. Spirit is ever available to fulfill itself as whatever is needed. Fulfilling whatever is needed and purposeful is the natural way.

Once again, turn away from the discords, disharmonies and inharmonious occurrences that exist through ego and the belief that you must flail about, whine, lament and struggle to survive. Let the way of Highest Good show itself.

Let the way manifest itself as to what is needed, and make every effort to understand that what is needed is not always what you, yourself, believe to be correct. Look to all that is perfection when you experience doubts and fears and know that must take place deeply within. That is the natural way, the way of attunement.

When the outer seems rocky, barren or in great turmoil, enter the Holy of Holies and consistently rise above the problem.

Never approach the problem at the level OF the problem, for that, in effect, mars the picture of perfection. Perfection can only be viewed in completeness and totality and, therefore, all problems must be viewed from above.

Indeed, you will see, for yourself, the insignificance of what appears to be the difficulty. Moreover, on the higher plane you enter into a more appropriate vibratory state, allowing the more positive circumstances and influences that always surround each soul to be made manifest.

This is impossible, or at best most difficult, if you persist in the gnashing of teeth, in whining and wailing that you are in distress, for that can only draw continued negativity to you.

So then, set aside the time, even in the midst of the most difficult travail, to go within and seek illumination and verification. Do so with a deliberate, heartfelt, prayerful attitude. Know that, if you will do this consistently and with some persistence, you will find, in every instance, a purposeful action will come to you and a greater way will open, smoothing out the apparent difficulty.

Know, then, that you do not need to retreat to the highest mountain to receive the benefit of illumination, or, for that matter, you need not withdraw from the daily difficulties that the unnatural man may experience.

Let the natural way be your way and make the rocky road smooth for you. The natural way is to view your personal color, to lovingly and graciously rise above the problem in meditation and let the greater spiritual way unfold for you. That is the harmonious and proper way of things and in accord with the universal good.

Know that all discord on the without is a way of letting you know that your attunement is fuzzy. That is to say, that greater efforts on your part are necessary to rise to the proper vibratory state and to allow you to participate more fully in all that is abundant and good.

Know that this is the most simple way and that Spirit is ever available to pour forth and eliminate the seeming difficulty, whether personal or impersonal, that you may face. Let us stress, once again, that this must be done with some diligence and persistence and, indeed, you must be willing to experience the greater good.

For, if you enjoy your tribulation, if you find that it brings you attention or in some way satisfies you, if you feel too much may be asked, or if you do not look for the greater way, you will find yourself stunted in growth and blocking the universal blessing that occurs throughout the Universe, minute by minute.

You need not beg and plead. Rather, attune yourself and do so lovingly. As you attune yourself, know that you enter into that experience which is perfection.

That experience of perfection can only bring you greater happiness, peace and a proper blessing. Let that avenue, then, of blessing and peace, be your way and know that is the natural way for you.

Turn, then, to the natural way for all your difficulties and know that there is no separation, nor has there ever been between you and your good, or for that matter, between you and your God. For the Lord is within and without and all about you. Within you, our friends, as an integral part of your heart and soul... spiritually flowing through you, minute by minute.

If that is true, then you must recognize that God's blessing is as intimate to you as the very breath of life you breathe. That is how very near the solution is to all that troubles you.

Do not let ego convince you that it knows the way, or that you must grasp and control the situation, for, as you release and rise above difficult circumstances they will, indeed, dissolve of their own accord. That includes all areas; financial, emotional, marital, relationships with others... certainly even extending to your plants, your pets, and the harmony within your dwelling. Know, then, that all these gracious matters are available to you and that Highest Good is the natural way.

Set aside the self indulgence of negativity, for that is merely what that is, self indulgence and self pity, except perhaps not seen by you in that light. Look to yourself and know that the willingness to set aside old and familiar difficulties requires that you step outside of yourself, leaving petty thoughts, beliefs and self indulgences behind.

Know, then, that all you need do is turn within, visualize your personal color and willingly set aside all you may consider needed in any given situation. In so doing, rise above the difficulty, openly and lovingly, and let the spiritual way, the correct way, flow forth, bringing to you a smoother, more clarifying way.

For clarity is the answer, our friends, but clarity must take place within and without. If you do not have clarity, you will find clarification always seen through the muddy window of ego and self indulgence, that the worldly mind is the way.

You might say, "How can that be true? How can God participate in such a personal way in the individual experience?" Heed our words: Spirit is within and without, all that is visible and invisible; Spirit is ever available, ever flowing forth. But many cover over that and an uncovering must be done.

That is to say, a recognition that Spirit is ever available is the act of uncovering; not only is Spirit available, but it is your most intimate companion, your most intimate resource, your most intimate way.

Do not try to perceive our Divine Father in the old ways that are familiar to you, or in some way categorize and familiarize yourself with what is Divine, for on the human plane, that is simply impossible. Divinity is difficult for the human plane of action to grasp.

You must know, for yourself, that spiritual experiences are actual and actualizing; that, indeed, it is the proper way to deal with your difficulties and that it is the way of peace and grace. All else is simply a subscribing to ego and the worldly mind, which, if you persist in that, at times in your experience the continuance of seemingly insurmountable difficulties will overwhelm you.

In time, indeed, the natural man experiences fewer difficulties and those that do arise encourage the practice of the principles that have been provided. The natural way is a recognition that there is no task too small for Spirit, nor too insignificant.

It is the recognition that your earthly experience is not divided into sections that are spiritual and non-spiritual, rather, that ALL is spiritual and that all solutions will come to you in a natural and spiritual way that is harmonious and proper.

Many are not ready to let go of their agonizing, fretting, whining and lamenting, or of their beastliness. But those of you who are able, will find that the spiritual way... the natural way... is indeed harmonious, peaceful and satisfactory, and that your greater good is ever available, ever flowing through you, around you, within and without.

If you doubt our words, put them to the test. Do as we have instructed and do so carefully, with reverence and diligence, and know that you will see the continuous demonstration of the truth and the propriety of our words.

The grace that flows through All will be immediately experienced by you.

So then, let this greater spiritual way unfold a happier path for you. Do not turn to that which is worldly, rather, turn to that which is peaceful, abundant and gracious.

Do these things, then, and let the natural way bless you from moment to moment, day to day, for that is the way of perfection and divinity. We say, then, do these things with a peaceful heart. Do them with persistence and diligence until they become, for you, a comfortable and natural way to receive the blessing that is ever present.

We say then, receive our blessing now. Amen.

* * * * * * *

CHAPTER 14

THE SPIRITUAL HEART

And so we have come to bring you our closing words and say to you, listen with deep attunement to what has been provided. Do not turn your back on this spiritual feast, but know that consistency and diligence are the watchword of the spiritual way.

If that is applied, it will bring you the flowing forth of the spiritual way which, indeed, is the flowing forth of peace, love, joy, happiness and of a greater way. Know, then, that resolution of all your difficulties, no matter how insignificant or how great, are available on the inner plane of action.

The way, then, is only achieved through diligent meditation and upliftment beyond the level of the problem, for, indeed, if you sink into the nature of the problem or, for that matter, below the problem itself, resolution in the spiritual way is most difficult.

Indeed, know that resolution lies in the higher plane and that comes to you in ways that may not be as you would have it. That, indeed, is a great blockage to spiritual living for, on some level, most individuals on your plane of action anticipate the conclusion of a difficulty and the final form it should take. That greatly limits Spirit, for Spirit flows forth for the highest good of all.

Spirit flows forth in an ever creative, abundant manner and can bring you many solutions from a difficulty, many avenues, not merely the limitations of what you may perceive as correct. Know that is truly the essence of the spiritual way, unrestricted flowing forth of Spirit, which can only take place with the cleansing of the heart and soul with forgiveness; with the frequent viewing of one's personal color, and, indeed, through the path of nonresistance.

That is to say, negative thinking, whining and lamenting, sinking to one's knees in worry and desolation are resistances to spiritual solutions and ways. Uplift yourself above that, as frequently as possible, that in doing so, all situations are greatly improved.

Know that, through faith and faith only, our Divine Father is ever with you, ever blessing you and ever available. This is the key to the Spiritual Heart for it is within the heart that the Intuitive Breath, the Holy Breath, itself, lodges.

That is, it is in that very area of mankind's expression, through love and devotion, that the creative way makes itself felt.

Know, then, that it is to love the Lord our God and to honor our Father, that you live the spiritual way, that you listen keenly to your intuition and understand that that is most valid.

This will require considerable retraining for many, for the worldly mind, indeed, says that intuition is an inaccurate way to function on your plane of action. That is entirely untrue, for a keen ear to intuition can bring you the highest solution possible, indeed, it is the creative way.

Do not turn to what is apparent, rather, turn within, and let the highest good express itself for all, for this is an immediate blessing and is your birthright and heritage. Our Divine Father is far too pure to express Himself in any other way.

Know that these words have been provided for all who will listen and all who will apply the principles as an alternative avenue to mysticism and other ways that may seem cumbersome and difficult for them. Our Father has heard the cries and has witnessed the efforts of so many to bring upliftment about, and that is, indeed, extraordinarily needed.

Let this way bring a greater unity in mankind, a greater expression of the Holy Breath and a greater outlet for all that is good, creative, and Holy.

Through each and every one of you who read our words and who are moved by them, know that this is your way, your true path, and that it is ever a blessing of peace, love, and grace to you. Let your faith be strong and diligent. Let your application of our principles be sure and true and know that you have come to a greater way for yourself.

Let these words bring you the assuredness and inner peace that is the hallmark of the uplifted consciousness. Let the way of our Lord Jesus Christ, the Buddha, and all Masters who have walked before you, come to you in clarity, guidance, inner peace and release.

Know that these are the blessings of the Spiritual Heart, that they are available, without reserve, to each of you who would apply the principles. Know that these words were graciously and lovingly provided for your use, your enjoyment and your greater spiritual expansion. Many already know that we are ever available, ever with you... you need only turn within.

Turn within with regularity, with consistency and with the heart open to the way of the Lord our God and let that way be your way. Let that way daily show you what is needed for you and know that what is needed may not always be as you have perceived it.

Let the greater way, in all matters, open forth for you, and let a greater love of our Divine Father and your brothers on your plane, come to you, for, indeed, all are One.

Know that mastership is available for you through our words. This will allow you a greatly uplifted way, bringing to all the essence of the spiritual way which is at the heart of the Universe, our friends, extending its loving presence forth now for all who would come to the presence of the Lord our God and for all who are willing to bless, to forgive and to set time aside daily to receive the impartation of the Holy Breath.

We say to you, then, receive our words in peace, love, clarity and spiritual purity, and know that the brotherhood of mankind is at hand. For, as you bless and forgive yourself and others, you will find that, in time, a greater closeness on the earth plane will evidence itself... and that is, indeed, the correct way for all. That is a true realization of spiritual understanding and, certainly, is the purpose of mastership.

So, then, be at peace and receive our blessing at this time. These, then, are our final words for this edition and they are offered in love and peace. Amen.

* * * * * * *

APPENDIX 1

Edgar Cayce channels through Diane 6/12/83 4:00 pm

Edgar Casey Session

A hallowed hello on this most auspicious and special occasion. We are all present for this meeting. Know that it is thru the opening of the Christ Consciousness in your heart and soul that has allowed this afternoon to be.

Do not be frightened for really very little will change for you during the course of this hour, except that you will leave greatly uplifted and that considerable insight into what it is to be in the service of the Father as a medium, trance medium, treatment reader or whatever other label human nature needs to apply.

The entity Edgar Casey lovingly awaits your great appearance in the next minute or two. We are taking you deeper than you ever have been before and ask that you relax into the loving arms of the Father and let this meeting unfold for you. Mr. Casey is about to begin. As he progresses, you may feel some slight vibrational changes, do not concern self with these. (Dede comments, somewhat softly.)

- - - - - - -

It is I, Edgar, we're here with you now our sister, Diane.

The purpose of this meeting is to help you achieve a greater awareness of what you have gained and to allay many of your fears, for I, too, struggled with many of the issues that you are currently making efforts to transcend.

When I initially began, I had no idea as to how to go about meditation as you were trained differently in the Eastern method, and now in the Christian method through your present teacher. Therefore, I merely would lay myself down on the couch, close my eyes and let the information come forth.

The problem for me was that this was an enormously difficult process because I did not understand the necessity to maintain top physical health, and to let the Father be the source of my supply.

In terms of income, I felt it necessary to do both as you are aware. Because of my very strict background, I felt that nothing could be given to me. In later years, I learned that all would be given to those in the service of the Father.

It is our objective today to provide you with some additional techniques as well as for me to let you know that I deeply concern myself with your growth and I am able to yet hark back to some of your issues, where I, too, feared a lack of accuracy, a lack of proper attitude, a lack of faith and, as you know, required the presence of others.

These fears, for one who agrees to take on such an enormous yoke, are initially only normal. There are certain ways in which you will learn to trust the validity of your readings. As you progress in this area, many of your fears will diminish. Again, I suffered many anxious moments and caused myself ill health, and my concern with personal integrity, at times, was overwhelming. We will begin now with the program for you to follow.

1. When you lie down to meditate. keep your body, as you do now currently, pointing North. Raise your consciousness a bit more and let the energy flow through you.

Initially. you should keep your arms at your sides, palms up, so that the total energy field around you can be elevated; by pressing your palms to your solar plexis you are turning the energy back within and, though this was the sort of thing you needed to do in the initial phases, it is not totally adequate.

As has been stressed in your many readings, nutritional balance, abstinence from very much alcohol, pursuit of your very excellent choice in physical exercises will greatly benefit you. Let God take over the area of your financial support, for, had I done this, I can certainly tell you that my life would have progressed more easily and certainly my family would have suffered less. As you do, and as all spiritual souls do, I, too, abstained from marital sexual relationship for the greater part of the time that I did readings.

Since my wife desired children there were periods in my life when sexual activity was permitted, followed by long hours of cleansing. Keep your arms relaxed and at the side of your body as flat as possible on the floor. The green light you see is telling you that the energy is flowing in a circle around you, which will greatly uplift your consciousness. You will find yourself more relaxed.

There will, of course, come a time when distractions like kitties lying upon you will be greatly reduced, but you seem to compensate for this very adequately. As you enter into your meditation, your preparations are adequate. We would suggest that perhaps a little food would be helpful to you, prior to meditation.

As you begin your readings this is the secret....you must begin to attune yourselves totally to the soul that you are reading for even if it is thine own soul, this is done by the visualization, at least initially, of a violet light, that is the light of mystical growth....so you will feel yourself surrounded by the green circle of light and the arc of the violet light should be crossing over your eyes as a bridge, for indeed that is precisely what it is - a bridge to the soul of another.

By this means, you will find that you will more easily attune self to the soul of another... in this way, the life direction and past life readings will be ever more accurate.

Do not be afraid to move about if necessary, for it took me many years to realize that it was possible to do so and still be in a very deep trance. A slight movement may make you greatly more comfortable than trying to rise above something distracting, as the Eastern philosophies will teach you.

As you move into your meditation, lift up your countenance to the face of God, open your heart as fully as you can and know that, in this way, nothing but truth can be perceived, nothing but truth will flow through you, nothing but truth will be given to you.

These techniques were developed over a period of years for me for, as, I have indicated, I merely would lie down and wait for the information to flow. But this was a very tedious process and there was a great deal of blocking which caused me certain physical difficulties. It is better to move into the trance state by means of careful preparation, visualization of the lights, calling upon the Christ and maintaining a relaxed but aligned position.

This will also benefit the spinal problems you came in with and help you to keep in greater alignment. Physical fitness can never be stressed too much. I, too, agree that someone as creative as you are needs an artistic outlet and feel that photography will provide you with even greater insights, for visualization and active imagination are a must in this work, for a dull mind could never pursue anything as abstract to most individuals as helping another by looking into his soul for hidden answers in the murky past lives.

As you photograph individuals, animals and your surroundings, you will find that you will come to an even greater understanding of the magnificence of the Father, as I, too, did. For, as each picture was developed and unfolded, I would see things in faces, and places that I had never before glimpsed. The possibilities for visualization, artistic outlet and consciousness expansion through photography are almost limitless. It is a fascinating way for you to pursue an additional avenue of spiritual growth.

The fears that lurk around you during the day, and just prior to meditation, are not only human fears, but fears of certain personality styles, brought up in the broadest (unable to understand word) of being good. This takes a long time to realize, for, as you are well aware, this information flows through you.

Nevertheless I perceive you doing as I did, fearing that you are not good enough for the undertaking at hand. Never give that another thought for it is a meaningless pursuit. As you know, in the eyes of the Father there is no good or bad there is only Isness. These anxieties are brought on by upbringing and personality and can only lead to frustration which is needful to be reduced in the life of one who serves.

2. In terms of employment, even though it was difficult to do both, and I still had negative feelings, I was not in such a formal and stringent setting as you. You will find that the release from this job or anything like it will uplift you far

beyond your expectations and help you in every aspect of your life and being.

You are now enjoying a very high level of meditation, the slight nausea you feel is not a necessity, it is simply your body's way of accustoming itself to a considerably raised vibrational level.

We would recommend that you not be too concerned with that either, for, as you step into your meditations with the proper physiological alignment, physical fitness, preparation and attunement with the Father, you will find that this is not a particularly difficult day, difficult way to pass your days.

If you find difficulty during the course of a reading, do not be afraid to ask for clarification for it is always given, only silently utter the words "clarification please" and you find that the matter is rephrased, or expressed in an entirely different way for your better reception. As you process through a reading and you feel that the reading is coming to a close and your vibrational level begins to slightly drop, invoke the white light, silently ask for Father's guidance throughout the day, minute to minute, and, as you bring yourself down, envision a lovely apricot color, for this is a very cooling color, a very soothing color and a color of At-Oness with the Father.

As you envision the apricot color, you will find that you will be able more readily to step out of a higher meditative state with less physiological rebound. I have received your thanks and know of your deep appreciation.

Another method that is most helpful, in terms of validity, if you have questions or concern that there is ego involved, do not be afraid to ask, silently, that ego be removed and merely ask for the rainbow, and, as you see the rainbow, you will know that the matters you are receiving are indeed true.

You are only humanly aware that your reception is superior, this has now been brought to your attention in order to keep you from struggling with ego, as well as some these personal issues that you have been pursuing. As you use these techniques you will find that your accuracy should be far beyond that of any medium who presently resides on the planet earth.

We are phrasing it in this way to allow you to comprehend what has transpired for you over the last year. I, too, was relatively afraid to admit that my gift was exceptional, that my abilities were more than most. As you know, yours are natural, mine were given. With assistance from time to time, you should be able to exceed the work I did, that is only a way to let you know not to be afraid, to continue on and know that you are very close to your goals, closer than even you fantasize.

3. Yes, the matter of transcription is an issue. Naturally, since I was reading long before the miracles of your electronic devices were discovered, a human secretary was required. This individual donated a great deal of her time out of love and forbearance due to my struggling financial position.

That will not be necessary in your case. The addition of a secretary for you is also due to your physiological size and the fact that you will be traveling to places that will require that you take some sort of luggage and handle certain business matters, do not resist, for it is well that need not bother yourself with these issues.

Your goal, as was mine, is to pursue At-Onement with the Father total openness to the Christ Consciousness and a willingness to lovingly provide others with your service and time, as the instrument through which the grace of the Father flows. Again, this is a major difference and one of the reasons I agreed to this meeting, for me in that time frame it seemed more of an affliction than the love of the Father expressing itself through me.

It took me many years of discipline and application to understand that this was indeed God's grace manifesting itself in my life. As you know, I was aware of the sacred nature of the work always, but I was unable to make the connection between grace and the sacred nature of the work, that too 'blunted' (that is what it "sounded" like) some areas of my life.

It is my concern that this work not deplete you as it did me, that you enter into it joyfully and graciously, that it bring you fulfillment and happiness for, in this way, you will be of total service to the Father. I am still learning my lessons, too, of obedience to the Father, although I have resided in spirit for some time, now, and find it certainly more desirable than the earthbound experience.

Your level of pursuit and understanding have contributed an upliftment and I wish to express my appreciation for this, for this, again, is a manifestation of an upraised consciousness. Others benefit. You already are aware that others benefit around you, others benefit unseen as well.

___ has benefited enormously by your growth. This is, indeed, important for you to understand, that while you are here you can be contributing to the upliftment of consciousnesses on both sides...this is not too often revealed for it would be misinterpreted by many. We feel that you will deal with this easily.

Know then that, with these steps, the physical fitness and the continued reduction in your resistance, your pursuit of the trance state will ever deepen. Although I was immediately into what is considered a trance state over the years, it grew in depth and breadth as it will too for you. Remember, ------------tape ran out ------------ (cough cough) that with the apricot light.

You will find that the absence of jewelry and light clothing will be most helpful to you. We would recommend (can't make out 2 or 3 words) for you, something other than the floor, but, for now, this is the most available and appropriate space in your dwelling. This well cushioned couch might be very conducive to your comfort which is extremely important when you are maintaining such a discipline.

Your work as a medical transcriber has been a tremendous benefit to you in learning to stay still for long periods of time, but, as you know, body position is all important. Do not concern yourself... the right couch will appear when there is need for you to have it.

Again, as you know, when I was directed to move I did, as you are preparing to do so now you will not believe what this move does for you, for I was simply aghast at the change in self. It is hard for those on the human plane to fully understand how severely a low vibrational area can affect you. You will find that the association of those on the path in an area that offers you cleaner air, along with the purity of cleaner minds will bring you into a greater fullness of understanding and happiness which can only benefit you as you pursue your work.

Since you will be traveling, you may need to practice, off and on, on the floor of your new dwelling for it is well not to become accustomed, too much, to one particular area, for that is nothing but a crutch. God is everywhere and so, too, is the information that will be necessary for you to receive. Trappings such as couches, garments, even the colors we recommended, are simply avenues, but they are not the totality, the Father is the totality.

We, on this side, agree that sufficient information has been provided for you. We are well pleased with your progress and with this meeting and your openness to it. You are already experiencing the cooling effect of the apricot light and reduction of vibrational level.

At this point, we think maybe one more additional meeting three weeks hence will be necessary, the time and date will be given. Your preparations will not have to be as extensive and if it does fall over your long weekend off, it will take place late on a Sunday afternoon and you will have the majority of the time to do as you wish.

Open your heart to every avenue that is being opened to you, for it is in this way that the hand of God can be realized in your life. I look forward to an opportunity to work with you again and once again wish to express my appreciation for the assistance you have given me, insights received and know that this, indeed, has been a reciprocal communication. Go now back into the world, and the dignity and the grace of the Father that is flowing into your life.

Your other friends bid you farewell until anon when we meet again.

Our blessings, peace and love go with you, our faithful daughter.

* * * * * * *

CPSIA information can be obtained
at www.ICGtesting.com
Printed in the USA
LVHW04s2335290918
591838LV00002B/19/P